省特色专业国金专业建设成果

省示范性中外合作项目国际金融专业建设成果

金融知识市民读本

Handbook of Financial Knowledge for Citizens

汪卫芳　姚星垣　孙　颖　著

浙江工商大学出版社 | 杭州
ZHEJIANG GONGSHANG UNIVERSITY PRESS

图书在版编目(CIP)数据

金融知识市民读本 / 汪卫芳,姚星垣,孙颖著.
—杭州:浙江工商大学出版社,2017.6
ISBN 978-7-5178-2176-2

Ⅰ.①金… Ⅱ.①汪… ②姚… ③孙… Ⅲ.①金融学
－基本知识 Ⅳ.①F830

中国版本图书馆 CIP 数据核字(2017)第 105777 号

金融知识市民读本
Handbook of Financial Knowledge for Citizens

汪卫芳　姚星垣　孙　颖　著

责任编辑	张莉娅　刘　韵
封面设计	许寅华
责任印制	包建辉
出版发行	浙江工商大学出版社
	(杭州市教工路 198 号　邮政编码 310012)
	(E-mail:zjgsupress@163.com)
	(网址:http://www.zjgsupress.com)
	电话:0571－88904970,88831806(传真)
排　　版	杭州朝曦图文设计有限公司
印　　刷	虎彩印艺股份有限公司
开　　本	710mm×1000mm　1/16
印　　张	11.75
字　　数	228 千
版 印 次	2017 年 6 月第 1 版　2017 年 6 月第 1 次印刷
书　　号	ISBN 978-7-5178-2176-2
定　　价	38.00 元

前　言

　　金融是现代经济的核心,其最基本的含义就是资金的流通。人们的生活始终离不开资金的流通和使用,资金流通最初和最基本的手段与工具是货币,但现代金融的基础是信用和清算体系。金融,不是高大上的特殊技巧,而是一种服务,一种社会所需要的服务。生活中时时刻刻存在着金融活动和金融交易,我们自身也在接触金融知识,体验着金融服务。信用有两个重要维度——时间价值和风险管理,可以说一切现代的金融工具、金融机构和金融市场都是围绕它们展开的。在现代经济社会,金融有效、安全的运作,一方面离不开对金融理论的深入探索,另一方面在实际层面则需要构建和完善金融制度。

　　本手册以通俗易懂的语言、生动形象的图片、浅显准确的英文带你进行一次金融之旅,让你可以在历史中感受金融的发展变化,在案例中体会金融对人们生活的重要意义,在体验中领略金融带来的魅力。

　　如果你还意犹未尽,那么,可以继续追踪本书参考书目的书刊资料进一步展开阅读,或者运用搜索引擎到网上冲浪,或者找专业领域的老师、朋友聊一聊……

　　希望了解金融知识、运用金融知识能够让你的生活更美好。

　　本手册也得到了课题组屠莉佳、王璐、吴蕴赟和徐冯璐等老师的大力支持,在此表示诚挚的谢意。由于水平有限,英文翻译和内容编排上难免存在一些不当之处,也敬请读者不吝赐教。

2016 年 12 月于杭州

目录
(Contents)

1 金融长廊 (Financial Gallery)

1.0 导言（Introduction） ·· 001

1.1 雅浦岛上的巨石（Huge Stones on Yap Island）·············· 002

1.2 雅典城邦的"六一农"（"One-sixth Peasants" of Athens Polis）········ 004

1.3 管子让齐桓公"替百姓还钱"（Guanzi Asked Duke Huan of Qi to Repay for the Common People）··································· 006

1.4 "汇通天下"的山西票号（Shanxi Exchange Banks） ·········· 010

1.5 荷兰的郁金香泡沫（Dutch Tulip Bubble） ················· 012

1.6 "银行的银行"——英格兰银行（"Bank of Banks"—the Bank of England）
··· 017

1.7 现代金融理论大爆炸（Big Bang of Modern Financial Theory）······ 021

2 货币史话 (Money Myth)

2.0 导言（Introduction） ·· 029

2.1 实物货币（Commodity Money） ························· 030

2.2 金属货币（Metallic Money）··························· 031

2.3 信用货币（Credit Money） ··························· 032

2.4 电子货币（Electronic Money） ······················· 032

2.5 货币职能（Function of Money） ····················· 033

2.6 "币"海拾遗（Stories Behind Currencies） ·················· 035

2.7 货币欣赏（Appreciation of Currencies） ·················· 050

3 支付漫说（Payment Stories）

3.0 导言（Introduction） ·· 054

3.1 货到付款（Cash on Delivery） ······························ 054

3.2 银行卡支付（Bank Card Payment） ······················ 063

3.3 第三方支付（Third-Party Payment） ······················ 077

3.4 转账支付（Wire Transfer Payment） ······················ 98

4 机构解密（Institution Decoding）

4.0 导言（Introduction） ·· 108

4.1 中央银行（Central Bank） ·································· 109

4.2 商业银行（Commercial Banks） ··························· 117

4.3 非银行金融机构（Non-bank Financial Intermediaries） ············ 122

5 百姓理财（Personal Financing）

5.0 导言（Introduction） ·· 132

5.1 股票与债券（Stocks and Bonds） ························ 132

5.2 基金（Funds） ··· 137

5.3 黄金与外汇（Gold and Foreign Exchange） ··············· 140

5.4 理财产品（Financial Products） ··························· 145

5.5 保险（Insurance） ·· 148

6 名人茶座（Celebrities' Salon）

6.0 导言（Introduction） ·· 151

6.1 现代经济学之父——亚当·斯密（Father of Modern Economics—Adam

Smith) ·· 152

6.2 古典经济学的完成者——大卫·李嘉图（Completer of Classical Economics—David Ricardo） ··································· 156

6.3 美国银行家——约翰·皮尔庞特·摩根（American Banker—John Pierpont Morgan） ······································ 159

6.4 宏观经济学创始人——约翰·梅纳德·凯恩斯（Founder of Macroeconomics—John Maynard Keynes） ···················· 163

6.5 股票之神——沃伦·爱德华·巴菲特（God of Stocks—Warren Edward Buffett） ·· 167

6.6 一般均衡理论创始人——里昂·瓦尔拉斯（Founder of the Marginal Revolution—Léon Walras） ···························· 171

6.7 微观经济学体系奠基人——阿尔弗雷德·马歇尔（Founder of Microeconomics System—Alfred Marshall） ·················· 173

6.8 美国第一位诺贝尔经济学奖获得者——保罗·安东尼·萨缪尔森（The First American Winner of the Nobel Memorial Prize in Economic Sciences—Paul Anthony Samuelson） ························· 175

Reference

1　金融长廊
（Financial Gallery）

1.0　导言（Introduction）

金融是什么？金融源自何时何处？

本章将带你漫步金融长廊，看看雅浦岛上古老的巨石货币和"现代信用体系"，聆听春秋时期管子的金融治国理念，感受1637年荷兰郁金香泡沫的疯狂，追溯作为现代金融基石的英格兰银行的崛起，见证盛极一时的山西票号的风云，领略现代金融理论大爆炸的魅力，反思21世纪初的金融海啸的影响……

What is finance? When and where did it come about?

In this chapter, you will have a happy financial meander by viewing the old stone moneys on Yap Island and "the modern credit system", listening to the ideas of finance governance proposed by Guanzi (Guan Zhong), a politician during the Spring and Autumn Period, feeling the the Dutch Tulip Bubble of 1637, tracing back to the rise of the Bank of England as the footstone of modern finance, witnessing the life of the has-been Shanxi Exchange Banks, surveying the charm of Big Bang of Modern Finance Theory, and introspecting hazards caused by financial Tsunami in the beginning of the 21st century...

今天，我们提起金融，可能马上就会联想到钱、信用卡、银行、股票，甚至还有余额宝和支付宝，等等。金融与我们的日常生活息息相关。可以想象没有金融的生活将是什么样的吗？如果让你生活在一个没有电或者没有金融的世界，你会选择哪个？

Whenever talking about finance，we may associate it with money，credit cards，banks and securities at once，even the Yu E Bao and Alipay virtual accounts，etc. Finance is closely bound up with our daily life. It is hard to imagine how we can live without finance. Which do you prefer，a world without electricity，or a world without finance?

那么，金融到底是什么？金融又是如何一步一步发展到今天的呢？我们不妨追根溯源，漫步金融长廊，寻找金融发展的轨迹。因为篇幅关系，我们只能在漫漫历史长河之中欣赏几朵浪花。我们首先从金融"天然的小伙伴"——货币说起。

Then，what is finance? How has finance developed to today's stage? Let's trace origins，meander the financial gallery and seek the track of financial development. Due to limited space，we can only appreciate several spindrifts in the long history by starting from the natural friend of finance—currency.

1.1 雅浦岛上的巨石 (Huge Stones on Yap Island)

雅浦岛是密克罗尼亚联邦的一个州，位于西太平洋上菲律宾群岛东南部。这么一个绝美而神秘的岛屿，堪称现代的世外桃源。岛上既有现代的教育，也有部落穿草裙的妇女。而最令人惊奇的是，它有世界上最大的货币：石币。

Yap Island is a state of the Federated States of Micronesia (FSM)，located in the southeast of the Philippine Islands in the Western Pacific，which is also called the Shangri-La for its gorgeous beauty and myth. There is modern education on the island，but even the tribe women wearing hula skirts. The most amazing is that the island has the biggest money in the world called stone money.

图 1　雅浦岛上的巨大石币

（Figure 1　Huge Stone Moneys on Yap Island）

这些石币最小的直径也有几十厘米，大的直径可达 3 米，厚 0.5 米，重达 4 吨。据说岛上最大的一个石币，需要 20 名成年男子才能搬动。很长一段时间里，石币都是本地的"流通货币"。

These stone moneys range from the smallest of dozens of centimeters in diameter to the big reachable to be three meters in diameter, with an half-meter thickness and a four-ton weight. It is said that the biggest stone money on the island needs 20 adult men to move. Stone money was the local currency in circulation for a considerably long period.

在看似原始的货币背后，却体现着十分现代的金融理念：货币的本质是什么？是交换媒介？是流通手段？这么巨大的石币显然难以"交换"和"流通"。事实上，雅浦岛上的居民只是把这些石币作为一个观念上的货币或者财富的代表。岛上人们之间的交易，往往是观念上达成交易，石币仍然放在原处。那么，这些石币到底反映了货币的什么本质呢？

Behind the seemingly original currency, it embodies a very modern financial philosophy. Then what is the nature of money? Is it the medium of exchange? Or means of circulation? It is obvious that so huge stone moneys are hard to either exchange or circulate. In fact, inhabitants on Yap Island just considered the stone money as representative of ideal currency or wealth. The deals between people on the island were also ideal ones while the stone moneys were still put where they were. Therefore, what the nature of money do they reflect on earth?

《货币野史》的作者菲利克斯·马汀说，雅浦岛上的石币，反映了货币作为信用和清算体系的本质。

Felix Martin, author of *Money*: *The Unauthorized Biography*, once said, the stone moneys on Yap Island reflected the natures of being credit and clearing system of money.

当岛上的居民相互了解和信任时,那么事实上货币本身的价值已经不重要了,就像现代的信用货币,本身不具备价值。到了电子货币,连有形的媒介也不需要了。

When inhabitants on the island understood and trusted each other, the value of money is actually of no importance, just like the modern credit money which also has hardly value itself. When electronic money is concerned, there is even no need to have visible medium.

货币从一般商品到特殊商品,再到观念货币,反映了金融演化的内在规律:金融的运行是基于信用的。随着现代信用体系的建立,金融的"虚拟性"就更加突出了。

The change of money from general merchandise to special merchandise and then to ideal money reflects the inherent law of financial evolution—the operation of finance is based on credit. With the establishment of modern credit system, the "virtuality" of finance is becoming more obvious.

1.2 雅典城邦的"六一农"("One-sixth Peasants" of Athens Polis)

金融的本质是信用,那么信用又是什么?

Since credit is the nature of finance, what is credit?

在孕育灿烂文明的古代雅典城邦,曾经出现过亚里士多德笔下的特殊公民——"六一农":借债者收成的六分之五要作为利息交给债主,自己只有六分之一。如果收成的六分之五还是不够缴纳利息,则债主有权在一年后把欠债的农民及其妻子儿女变卖为奴。

In classical Athens Polis where glorious civilization was breeded, special citizens called "One-sixth Peasants" in Aristotle's writings appeared: The five-sixths of the harvest of borrowers should be given to the lenders as interest, while they themselves could only keep one-sixth. If the five-sixths of the harvest was not enough for them to pay for the interest, the lenders had the rights to sell the peasant and his wife and children as servants one year later.

图 2 古希腊雅典城邦遗址
(Figure 2 Site of Athens Polis of Ancient Greek)

"六一农"的悲惨经历告诉我们:第一,当某人现在的资源(货币)不够时,可以(甚至必须)向资源有多余的人借用;第二,这种借贷是以偿还本金和支付利息为代价的;第三,借贷存在一定的风险,如果不能还本付息怎么办?

The miserable experience of "One-sixth Peasants" shows several points to us. Firstly, when one doesn't have enough present resources (currency), he can (even must) borrow from those who have redundant resources. Secondly, this kind of borrowings is finished at the cost of paying back principal together with interest. Thirdly, there exist some risks when the borrowing happens, for example, what if the borrower can not repay the principal and interest?

第一条,即金融的通俗定义——资金的融通:资金从供给方转移到需求方。第二条,说明金融的本质特性之一——时间价值。即金融活动不是免费的,对资金需求方而言需要额外支付价值,就是所谓的"时间价值"或者"利息"。第三条,说明金融活动的本质特性之二——风险。理论上金融活动或多或少都存在风险,因此需要某种技术去保障,可以是形式的或者实质的。风险管理成为现代金融的核心。

The first point above mentioned is referred as the common definition of finance, namely, the financing of capital which is transferred from suppliers to demanders. The second point illustrates one of the essential natures of finance—time value, that is financial activities are never free, and demanders have to pay additional value that is called "time value" or "interest". The third point illustrates the second nature of financial activities—risk. There exist certain risks for financial activities theoretically which need some technology either formal or essential to protect.

Therefore, risk management becomes the core of modern finance.

顺便说一句,保障的方式有很多种,但最常见的方式有两种,一种是以现有资产作为抵押,另一种就是以未来的预期收入作为担保。而现代常见的购房按揭贷款则是这两者的结合:一方面把要买的房子抵押给银行,一旦没有能力还贷款,银行就有权出售房子来收回资金;另一方面贷款人也需要开收入证明,这是在向借钱给他的银行保证,他会用未来的收入偿还贷款。

By the way, there are many different ways to protect financial activities, but two of which are most common. One is to pledge against present assets, the other is to guarantee against future expected income. The common way called mortgage loan nowadays is the combination of the above two ways. On the one hand, the borrower has to make the house he is going to buy as a mortgage to the bank who has the right to sell the house for the loan when the borrower can't repay the loan; on the other hand, the borrower has to submit his income certificate which promises the bank that the borrower will repay the loan by his future income.

1.3 管子让齐桓公"替百姓还钱"(Guanzi Asked Duke Huan of Qi to Repay for the Common People)

金融活动的基石在于信用,而信用的形式是多种多样的。现在我们把目光投向中国古代春秋时期。

The footstone of financial activities is credit which has various forms. Now, let's turn our eyes to the Spring and Autumn Period of ancient China.

当时的齐国高利贷盛行,农民负担很重。齐桓公①在管子②的建议下,派大臣分别到全国各地调查放贷情况。大臣们调查完毕回来,报告说全国所有高利贷者,共放债三千万钱,三千万钟左右的粮食,借债贫民有三千多家。管子说:"不料我国

---

① 齐桓公,春秋五霸之首,公元前685—前643年在位,春秋时代齐国第十五位国君,姜姓,吕氏,名小白,是姜太公吕尚的第十二代孙。桓公任管仲为相,推行改革,实行军政合一、兵民合一的制度,齐国逐渐强盛。当时中原各诸侯苦于戎狄等部落的攻击,于是齐桓公打出"尊王攘夷"的旗号,北击山戎,南伐楚国,成为中原第一个霸主。

② 管子,姬姓,管氏,名夷吾,谥敬。管子是春秋时期法家的代表人物,是中国古代著名的哲学家、政治家、军事家,被誉为"法家先驱"等。

的百姓，等于'一国之内有五个国君在征敛'①，这样还想国家不穷，军队不弱，怎么可能呢？"

At that time, usurious loans were prevailing in Qi (one of the kingdoms in the Spring and Autumn Period), making a heavy burden on peasants. Duke Huan of Qi took the advice by Guanzi and appointed ministers to survey the lendings in different areas throughout the kingdom. The result of the survey showed that all the usurers in the kingdom lended thirty million Qian (a kind of currency in circulation at that time) and about thirty million Zhong (a kind of the ancient measuring tool at that time) of grains, and there were more than three thousand poor peasant borrower families. Guanzi said, "It is surprised that the people in our country have to pay the tax as much as that of five kingdoms. How can it be possible that the people will become rich and the army become strong?"

桓公问怎么办，管子就叫他下号令："前来朝拜贺献的，都须献来织有漂亮花纹的美锦。"于是，美锦的价格就上涨了，而在国库"栈台"所藏的同类美锦，价格也随着涨了许多倍。然后，国君下令召见高利贷者，并设宴招待他们。

Then Duke Huan of Qi asked how to solve the problems. Guanzi asked him to order that those who came to worship and pay contribute must present beautiful brocades with pretty arabesquitic. As a result, the prices of the beautiful brocades rose, so did the prices of the same brocades in the national treasury also increase by many folds. Then, the Duke called in the usurers and gave a banquet to entertain them.

太宰敬酒后，桓公便提衣起立，问："我需要用钱的事情很多，只好派官在国内收税。听说诸位曾把钱、粮借给贫民，使他们得以完成纳税义务。我藏有漂亮花纹的美锦，每匹价值万钱，我想用它来为贫民们偿还本息，使他们免除债务负担。"

After the prime minister proposed a toast, Duke Huan of Qi stood up and asked those at the feast, "I have lots of things that need to do with money, so I have to collect taxes throughout the country. It is said that you once lend money or grain to the poor to help them fulfil the tax obligation. Now, I have many beautiful brocades with pretty arabesquitic, each of which values ten thousand Qian, and

---

① 一个国君征税，四大家族盘剥百姓，所以相当于有五个国君征税，百姓不堪重负，纷纷向高利贷者借债。

I want to use them to repay the principals and interests for the poor and help them free from the debt burden."

高利贷者都俯首下拜说："君上如此关怀百姓,请允许我们把债券捐献于堂下。"

All the usurers bowed their heads and replied, "Dear Monarch, you are so concerned about the common people, just allow us to leave the debentures here."

桓公又说："那可不行。诸位使我国贫民春得以耕,夏得以耘。我感谢你们,无所奖励,你们连这点东西都不肯收,我心不安。"

"No, no, I can't agree." said Duke Huan of Qi. "You help the paupers in our country till/sow in spring, weed clearing in summer. I should thank you for your deed, but I don't have anything else. I will feel worried if you even refuse to accept the brocades."

这样,国家拿出的织锦不到三千匹,便偿清了四方贫民的本息,免除了他们的债务。贫民对君王自然更感激不尽。从此,齐国经济上空前地焕发了活力,人民拥护国家和君王,齐国政治上稳定,军事上也空前地强大起来。

Thus, Duke Huan of Qi only took out less than three thousand brocades to repay the debts of the poor peasants and helped them free from debts. The poor people were very appreciated to the Duke and all of them supported the kingdom and the Duke with vitality which also sparkled the economy of the country. The kingdom of Qi entered an unprecedentedly stable and powerful period.

这就是历史上著名的"美锦谋"。从金融和信用的角度看,第一,它体现了个人信用与国家信用的转换。在这个过程中,表面上是用国王的"私房钱"替贫民还贷款,不得罪富人(高利贷者、贷款人),又直接有利于贫民(借贷人)。第二,巧妙利用资产价格泡沫完成信用交换。先利用国家力量(规定贡品),把织锦的价格拉高很多倍,再由国君出面,宴请富豪,用织锦为百姓还债。第三,资产泡沫的标的是"美锦",在当时是贡品,属于奢侈品,对一般老百姓影响不大。

This was the famous "Strategy of Beautiful Brocades" in history. From the point of view of finance and credit, we can get three points. Firstly, it embodies the switch of personal credit and national credit. In the story, Duke Huan of Qi seemingly used his cheeseparing to repay the loans for the paupers without offending the rich (usurers and lenders), and benefiting the poor peasants (borrowers). Secondly, the asset price bubble was subtly used to finish the credit interchange. Above all, Duke Huan made the best use of national power (stipulated tribute) to draw highly the price of brocades, then repaid the debts for the poor by means of feting the rich on behalf of the Duke. Thirdly, as the object of the asset bubble, brocades were articles of tribute and also luxuries at that time, so the increase of their price wouldn't impact greatly on the common people.

图 3　春秋时期的名相管子

(**Figure 3 Guanzi—Famous Minister of the Spring and Autumn Period**)

这个故事似乎有种劫富济贫的味道，不过因为计划周密，执行到位，既得利益者（高利贷者）并没有直接反弹，可见管子对人性把握之深和实施艺术之高超。

This story seems to have a sense of robbing the rich and assisting the poor. With the careful plan and good execution, it didn't offend the people with vested interest (usurers), which showed the super skills of Guanzi to understand the humanity and carry out the plan.

管子的经济金融思想广泛而深邃，又与实践紧密结合。耶鲁大学著名金融学教授对管子的思想也敬佩不已①。如果你对此感兴趣，不妨读一读《管子》，说不定对个人理财颇有启发，对各国经济金融政策的理解也会有所加深。

The financial thought of Guanzi was profound which was also closely integrated with practice. Even the famous financial professor of Yale University admired him

---

①　"2000 年中的一天，在耶鲁校园里的一条街上，我碰到 William Goetzmann，他当时正手拿一本书，兴冲冲地从邮局往办公室走。见到我，便高兴地把书摆在我的眼前，说：'你看看，这是齐国管子的经济著作，他说到的关于齐国货币政策、公债举措，是多么精辟呀！'"转引自陈志武为《价值起源》一书所作的序言。

very much. If you have some interest, you can read the book *Guanzi* which may enlighten you on personal financing and make you better understand the economic and financial policies of different countries.

1.4 "汇通天下"的山西票号(Shanxi Exchange Banks)

票号又叫票庄或汇兑庄,是一种专门经营汇兑业务的金融机构,盛于清朝。

Exchange banks(for exchange and transfer of money), also called money shops or exchange shops, were a kind of financial institution specialized in exchanging businesses. Exchange banks thrived in the Qing Dynasty.

一般而言,现代金融活动似乎不受地域限制,敲几个键盘,就能完成资金从地球一端到另一端的转移,而且几乎是瞬间完成。不过在漫长的金属货币时期,资金的转移就没有这么方便了。

Generally speaking, modern financial activities have no geographic restrictions; they can transfer funds successfully from one end of the Earth to the other end almost within a second only by clicking the keyboard. But during the long period of metallic currency, it was not so convenient to transfer funds.

在我国明清时期,随着商品经济的发展,跨区域的贸易日益发达,而携带大量的金银货币十分不便,又不安全。票号办理汇兑、存放款,解决了运送现银的困难,加速了资金周转,促进了商业繁荣。

During the period of the Ming and Qing Dynasties in China, transregional trade increasingly developed with the development of commodity economy. It was neither convenient nor safe for people to carry a large amount of gold or silver money. Exchange banks conducted businesses of exchange, deposit or loans, which not only solved the problems in transporting money, but also speeded the turnover of funds, thus promoting the business boom.

票号由山西商人首创,随着票号业的发展,山西商人逐渐执中国金融界之牛耳[1]。同时,由于商业资本与金融资本的结合,山西商人成为当时国内商业和金融界一支举足轻重的力量。这是经济发展与金融发展相互促进的一个典型的例子。

Exchange banks were first set up by merchants in Shanxi Province. With

---

[1] 曲殿元在《中国金融与汇兑》(上海大东书局 1930 年版)中说:"山西票庄执中国金融界之牛耳,约百余年。"

the development of exchange shops，Shanxi merchants played a leading role in the whole Chinese financial circle. Meanwhile，they became an important force of domestic commerce and financial circle because of the combination of commercial and financial capital. It was also a typical example of mutual promotion between economic and financial development.

图4 "汇通天下"的山西票号
（Figure 4 Shanxi Exchange Banks）

值得一提的是，早于票号出现的钱庄和票号的业务内容与活动地区是有区别的。钱庄的主要业务是对商人办理存放款项，间或经营地区之间的商业汇兑，所以和商业的联系比较密切。票号是以汇兑为专业的，有放款，但也只贷给钱庄而不贷给一般商人。

It is worthy of mentioning that the businesses and activity regions of the money houses（old-style Chinese private banks）which appeared earlier than exchange banks were different from that of exchange banks. The main businesses of money houses were handling deposits for businessmen and sometimes operated the businesses of regional commercial exchange. Therefore，money houses had closer relations with commerce. Exchange banks specialized in exchange（transfer of funds），and also made loans but only to money houses instead of normal businessmen.

从这个角度看，钱庄承载的金融活动更具有本地性，而票号背后的金融活动则更具有跨区域性质。不过，现代金融业的发展并没有完全消除"区域性"金融机构存在的"土壤"。"社区银行"、信用社、城市商业银行等地方金融机构由于对本地客户在服务内容和服务形式需求的了解上具有一定的信息优势，因此只要无法完全消除这种信息不对称，地方中小金融机构将仍然有其生存的土壤和空间。这就像

图5 山西票号代表性人物乔致庸的故居"乔家大院"

(Figure 5 Qiao's Grand Courtyard—the Former Residence of Qiao Zhiyong Who Was the Representative Figure of Shanxi Exchange Banks)

尽管面临大超市的挑战,社区便利店依然有生存空间一样。

Viewed from this angle, financial activities conducted by money houses possessed more locally, while those behind exchange banks are more trans-regional. However, the development of modern financial industry by no means entirely eliminated "soil" for "regional" financial institutions. Local financial institutions such as community banks, credit cooperatives and city commercial banks have information advantages in the understanding of local clients' demands for service items and patterns, so, they will still have the space and foundation to develop because this kind of information asymmetry can't be completely eliminated. It is just like the community convenience stores can also have their chances even facing the challenges of supermarkets.

1.5 荷兰的郁金香泡沫(Dutch Tulip Bubble)

如果说称霸世界一时的荷兰,衰败的原因竟然是小小的郁金香,或许有点耸人听闻,但是在这个事件背后的金融因素却绝对不容忽视。

It is probably somewhat lurid that Dutch—once a country dominating the world—declined because of the teeny-weeny tulips, but the financial factors behind this event can be neglected by no means.

下面就通过"郁金香泡沫"这个耳熟能详的故事来说说金融与大国兴衰这个"宏大命题"。

Hereafter, let's discuss a "grand proposition" about the finance and the rise and decline of a great power by means of a very familiar story called Tulip Bubble.

荷兰人十分喜爱郁金香。但是当这种喜爱在金钱利益的驱使下过了头，就变得疯狂而危险了，甚至将会演变成一场灾难。苏格兰历史学家查尔斯·麦凯在其研究投机及脱离理智行为的经典著作《惊人的流行妄想回忆录》中，对荷兰的郁金香投机狂潮做了十分贴切的描述：1636 年，由于郁金香珍贵品种的需求量不断增长，阿姆斯特丹、鹿特丹、莱顿、哈莱姆及其他一些城市的股票交易场所设置了定期的销售市场。人们围着小小的郁金香球茎团团转，一个个充满了自信……如同其他的期货交易一样，投机商操纵着郁金香市场的行情，他们趁价格下跌时建仓，大量囤积，转手就能获取暴利。许多人转眼之间就成了巨富……一切就像一只悬挂着的金饵，诱惑着人们一个一个涌向郁金香交易场所。那种情形，犹如蜜蜂围着糖罐一般。几乎所有的人都坚信郁金香热会永远持续下去，无论是王公贵族，还是一般的市民、农民、艺人、海员、脚夫、仆人，甚至烟囱清扫工和洗衣老妇都纷纷投身于郁金香热。此时连最愚钝迟缓的人都加入进来，体味一夜暴富的喜悦。

The Dutch were fond of tulip very much, but just because of the overzealous keen on tulip for pecuniary benefit, it became crazy and dangerous even would turn into a disaster. In his classics *Extraordinary Popular Delusions & the Madness of Crowds* which researched speculation and behaviors devoid of rationality, Scotland historian Charles Mackay gave a proper description on Holland Tulip Speculation Mania: In 1936, periodical sales markets were set up in stock trading places in Amsterdam, Rotterdam, Leiton, Harlem and other cities because of the increasing demand for rare types of tulips. People were full of confidence and keened on the small tulip bulbs... Just like other futures trading, the speculators controlled the markets of tulip, they bought in and hoard for speculation when the prices went down, passed on and made sudden huge profits. A lot of people became millionaires overnight... All was like a hanging gold lure tempted more and more people rush into tulip trading places just as bees flied around sugar bowls. Almost all people were sure that the tulip mania would last forever. Either the nobility or ordinary citizens, peasants, artists, seamen, porters and servants, even the chimney sweeps and old laundry women all threw themselves into the tulip mania one after another. At that time, even the stupidest people joined the crazy to experience the happiness of becoming rich overnight.

1637 年，郁金香的价格已经涨到了不可思议的地步，例如，一种名贵的"永远的奥古斯都"①的郁金香售价高达 6700 荷兰盾，这个价格足以买下阿姆斯特丹运河边的一幢豪宅，而当时荷兰人的平均年收入只有区区 150 荷兰盾。

In 1637, the price of tulip had increased to an incredible extent, for example, a rare kind tulip named "Forever Semper Augustus" was sold at a high price of 6,700 Dutch guilders which was enough to buy a villa along the Amsterdam Canal. However, the average yearly income of the Dutch then was only 150 guilders.

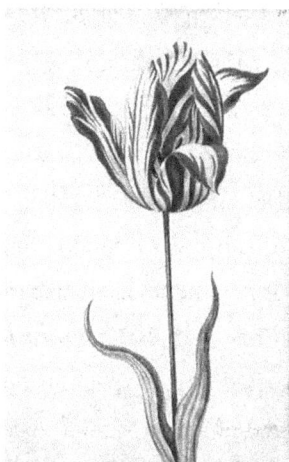

图 6　郁金香中的传奇——"永远的奥古斯都"
(Figure 6　Tulip Legend—Forever Semper Augutus)

随着热度不断攀升，荷兰人脱离郁金香球茎实体，开始了郁金香球茎的期货交易，期货合同在荷兰各地被炒得热火朝天。其他国家的欧洲人也被荷兰人的狂热弄得晕头转向，纷纷涌入荷兰参与交易。

With the rising heat, the Dutch began futures trading on tulip bulbs devoid of the real trading. Futures contracts were speculated all over the Holland. Europeans from other countries were also confused and disoriented by the Hollanders' craze and swarmed into Holland to trade.

---

① "永远的奥古斯都"是一种具有凌乱羽衣的红色与白色的郁金香，其花瓣上附有红白相间的花纹。据说真正的"永远的奥古斯都"品种现在已经绝种，其价值远比黑色郁金香更为昂贵。"永远的奥古斯都"花瓣上的条纹是花叶病的病毒基因造成的，所以极难栽培。

到了 1637 年 2 月，倒买倒卖的人逐渐意识到郁金香交货的时间就快要到了。人们开始怀疑，花这么大的价钱买来的郁金香球茎就是开出花来到底能值多少钱？前不久还奇货可居的郁金香合同一下子就变成了烫手的山芋。持有郁金香合同的人宁可少要点价钱也要抛给别人。

However，these who made speculative buyings and sellings gradually realized the delivery time of tulip was approaching till February，1637. People started to doubt how much on earth the flowers would value for they spent so much money buying the bulbs. The rare tulip contracts not long before suddenly became thorny "sweet potato". Those who held contracts were eager to undersell them.

在人们信心动摇之后，郁金香价格立刻就开始下降。价格下降导致人们进一步丧失对郁金香市场的信心。持有郁金香合同的人迫不及待地要脱手，可是，在这个关头很难找到"傻瓜"。恶性循环的结果导致郁金香市场全线崩溃。

When people's confidence started to shake，the prices of tulip decreased right away，which further weakened the confidence of the people. Those who held the contracts were anxious to get away the contracts but it was so difficult to find "the big fool" at the particular moments. The vicious circle resulted in the complete collapse of tulip markets.

郁金香泡沫的高峰期仅仅持续了一个多月。由于许多郁金香合同在短时间内已经多次转手买卖且尚未交割完毕，最后一个持有郁金香合同的人开始向前面一个卖主追讨货款，这个人又向前面的人索债。荷兰的郁金香市场顿时从昔日的景气场面变成了凄风苦雨和逼债逃债的地狱。

The peak season of Tulip Bubble only lasted for more than one month before it fell through. Since the contracts were transferred several times in a short period and had not been delivered, the last holder began to recover the payment for goods from the second-last seller，and the second-last seller claimed the debts from his prior party accordingly. In the end，the Dutch tulip markets which were booming in the past suddenly became the distressed hell where people pressed payments for debts and evaded debts.

1637 年 4 月 27 日，荷兰政府决定终止所有的合同。一年之后，荷兰政府通过一项规定，允许郁金香的最终买主在支付合同价格的 3.5% 之后终止合同。郁金香事件还沉重打击了荷兰经济，使这个曾经繁荣一时的经济强国开始走向衰落。

The Dutch government decided to terminate all the contracts on April 27, 1637. One year later, the government passed a regulation to permit the last buyer of the contract could terminate the contract after he paid 3.5% of the contract price. The tulip event also heavily hit the economy and led the once economic power to decline.

关于郁金香泡沫的警示,至少有以下几点:

When it comes to the heritage of the Tulip Bubble, there are several points as follows:

第一,让世人见识了金融投机的巨大威力。金融投机的背后,是对理性人假设的质疑和挑战,这是当今金融研究中的重要分支——行为金融理论①的逻辑基础;人并不总是理性的,甚至常常是非理性的,面对过度投机产生的泡沫,往往在羊群效应的驱使下,飞蛾扑火一般使泡沫越来越大,直至破灭。

Firstly, the event let the people all over the world experience the giant power of finance speculation behind which was the query and challenge on hypothesis of rational man, the logic basis of behavioral financial theory, an important branch of modern financial research. Human beings can not be rational all the time, they may even be very irrational from time to time when facing the bubbles of overspeculation, and they were usually impelled by herd behaviors and made the bubble bigger and bigger like "A moth flutters about the light" and at last fell through.

第二,金融工具的创新。郁金香泡沫催生了衍生金融产品:期货。期货通俗地说就是买卖双方通过协议约定将来按照特定的价格进行某种商品的交易。这里的风险就在于价格风险,因为将来的价格是不确定的,即可能高于期货价格,也可能低于期货价格。按照约定的价格进行交易,既有可能大赚一笔,也有可能血本无归②。

Secondly, the creation of financial instrument is made. The Tulip Bubble created a financial derivative: Futures. In a more popular saying, futures refers

---

① 2013年诺贝尔经济学奖得主罗伯特·希勒就是研究行为金融的先驱者之一。希勒不仅撰写专业论文功力深厚,写起带有科普性质的畅销书的水平也同样十分了得。他的《非理性繁荣》一书成为行为金融领域科普读物中的经典。

② 另外,期货合约可以买,也可以卖。比如约定1个月后以100荷兰盾的价格卖某种郁金香,如果3个月后降价了,那么可以从市场低价买入,再在期货市场高价卖出,同样可以赚钱。这意味着方向判断对了,价格涨跌都可以赚钱,反过来判断错了,价格涨跌都会赔钱,这对专业要求就十分高了。

to the trade in which the buyer and seller trade a certain commodity in the future at the given price appointed in the agreement. The risk here was price risk because the price in the future is uncertain—possibly higher or lower than the futures price. Deals done at the appointed price may mean a big profit or a loss of all money.

第三，金融发展与经济增长的关系。没有实体经济支撑的金融是脆弱的，而当这种没有实体经济支撑的金融急剧膨胀时，就变得十分危险了。当全民疯狂之时，离最后的崩溃就不远了。

Thirdly, the event let us know the relationship between financial development and economic growth. Finance would become fragile without the support of real economy. It would be very dangerous when this kind of finance expanded rapidly. It is also near the last collapse when all the people are crazy.

郁金香泡沫虽然已经十分遥远了，但是，类似的历史仍然一次次固执地在世界各地上演，包括互联网泡沫、房地产泡沫、金价泡沫等，似乎没有尽头。这也许在于金融"难懂"的根本原因：金融投机和泡沫的背后，是复杂的人性。

Though it was long ago when the Tulip Bubble happened, the similar history still took place time and time again all over the world, including internet bubble, real estates bubble and gold bubble, etc., and it seems there is never an end. It maybe lies in the root cause of "difficult finance": behind the financial speculation and bubble is the complicated humanity.

1.6 "银行的银行"——英格兰银行（"Bank of Banks"—the Bank of England）

英格兰银行成立于1694年，早期的英格兰银行只是英国政府的"钱袋子"。当时庞大的战争开支早已将英国政府的财政收入消耗一空。为筹集更多军费，急需用钱的英国国王和议会迅速采纳了一位叫威廉·佩特森的苏格兰商人的提议——成立一家可向政府贷款的银行。于是，1694年7月27日，伦敦城的1268位商人合股出资，正式组建了英格兰银行。此后的短短11天内，英格兰银行就为政府筹措到120万英镑的巨款，极大地支持了英国在欧洲大陆的军事活动。

The Bank of England was set up in 1694, and it was only the government's pocket in its early period. At that time, the huge war expenses consumed up the

British government's fiscal revenue. In order to raise more military expenditure，the King of England and his parliament who were badly in need of money adopted the suggestion of a Scottish merchant named William Peterson to establish a bank which could make loans to the government. So，1,268 merchants in London contributed funds jointly and set up the Bank of England on July 27, 1694. In eleven days after the establishment，the Bank of England raised a huge amount of 1.2 million pounds for the government and greatly supported its military activities in the continent of Europe.

除了经营一般的商业银行业务——发行钞票、吸收存款、发放贷款，英格兰银行一开始就与政府维系着一种特殊而密切的关系———一直向政府提供贷款，负责筹集并管理政府国债，还逐渐掌握了绝大多数政府部门的银行账户。据此，英格兰银行的实力和声誉迅速超越了其他银行。到 1837 年，英格兰银行不但安然挺过了当年的银行危机，还拿出大笔的资金，帮助那些有困难的银行渡过难关，这也成为英格兰银行充当"最后贷款人"角色的开始。

Besides the ordinary commercial banks' businesses such as issuing banknotes, attracting deposits and making loans, the Bank of England has maintained a special and close relationship with the government from the very beginning to make loans for the government ever since，take charge to raise funds and manage government's bonds, and gradually grasped the bank accounts of most of the government's departments. Hereby，the power and reputation of the Bank of England surpassed other banks promptly. Up to 1837, the Bank of England had not only survived safely the bank crisis and also took out a large sum of money to help those banks in difficulties to pull through, which was the beginning of the Bank of England becoming to play the role of "lender of last resort".

到了 1844 年，英国议会通过《银行特许法》，让英格兰银行在发行钞票方面享有许多特权。自此，英格兰银行逐渐退出一般性的商业银行业务，专注于货币发行，并开始承担维护英国金融市场稳定和监督其他商业银行的职能。1928 年，英国议会通过《通货与钞票法》，使英格兰银行垄断了在英格兰和威尔士地区的货币发行权。到 1946 年，英国议会通过《英格兰银行法》，赋予英格兰银行更为广泛的权利，使它可以按照法律对商业银行进行监督和管理（后来这项职能移交给 1997 年 10 月成立的金融服务局），英格兰银行终于名正言顺地成为英国的中央银行。

In 1844，British Parliament passed *the Bank Charter Act*，granted the Bank of England many privileges on issuing banknotes. From then on，the Bank of England gradually gave up common commercial businesses，specialized in issuing money and started to undertake the functions of maintaining the stability of British financial market and supervising other commercial banks. In 1928，British Parliament passed *the Currency and Bank Notes Act*，helping the Bank of England monopolize the right to issue paper money over England and Wales. In 1946，British Parliament passed *the Bank of England Act*，giving the Bank of England more extensive rights to supervise and manage commercial banks according to laws（this function was turned over to Financial Service Bureau in October，1997）. The Bank of England eventually became the central bank of England.

图 7 "银行的银行"——英格兰银行
（**Figure 7** "**Bank of Banks**"—**the Bank of England**）

英格兰银行的诞生和发展，留给我们的思考至少包括以下几点：

What we can reflect on from the birth and development of the Bank of England can be listed as follows：

第一，金融制度的建立非一朝一夕之功。英格兰银行最初是一家普通的商业银行，因当时国内外政治、经济形势的需要，逐步转型为国家的银行、银行的银行和发行的银行，标志着金融和信用的国家属性地位的日益确立。可以说英格兰银行是现代国家宏观调控及货币政策的起点和源头，是当今世界包括美联储在内的各国中央银行的鼻祖和模范。

Firstly，the establishment of financial system can not be built in one day. The Bank of England was initially a common commercial bank which gradually turned into a national bank because of the need of political and economic situation in and out of the country. National bank, bank of banks and bank of issue symbolized the statehood position of finance and credit had been established day by day. It can be said that the Bank of England is the origin and source of modern state macro-control and monetary policy, and it is also the originator and model of central banks all over the world including the Federal Reserves (FED).

第二,从现代的眼光看,金融制度的构建也许并非出于本意。经过漫长的斗争,1688 年光荣革命以后,英国国王、地主、新兴资产阶级等国内各种政治力量达到相对均衡,而应对荷兰、法国的战争的威胁和挑战,就变得至关重要。随着英格兰银行作为中央银行地位的逐渐确立,英格兰的金融市场有了大发展,有效地满足了对外战争的资金需求。

Secondly, from the modern viewpoint, the construction of financial system probably was not the original idea. After the lengthy war and especially the Glorious Revolution in 1688, the different civil political power within England including the King of England, the landlords and the newly-developing bourgeoisie gradually reached a relative equilibrium, while it became more and more important to face the menace and challenge from the wars against Holland and France. With the establishment of the Bank of England as the central bank, the English financial market developed rapidly and effectively satisfied the capital need for foreign wars.

第三,一项金融制度不可能完美无缺,曾经助推英国成为"日不落"帝国的英格兰银行也不是不可战胜。例如 1992 年索罗斯成功狙击英格兰银行事件,表明中央银行也不是万能的。在这场捍卫英镑的行动中,英格兰银行动用了价值 269 亿美元的外汇储备,但最终还是遭受惨败,被迫退出欧洲汇率体系。英国人把 1992 年 9 月 15 日——退出欧洲汇率体系的日子称作"黑色星期三"。

Thirdly, there is not a financial system which is flawless, even the Bank of England who ever helped boost the United Kingdom to become a big empire——"on which the sun never set" was not invincible. The event of George Soros successfully sniped the Bank of England in 1992 indicated that central banks were not all-powerful. In the war to defend pound, the Bank of England employed foreign exchange reserves of 26.9 billion dollars, but finally suffered a disastrous defeat and was forced to retreat from the European Exchange Rate System. The British called September 15, 1992 Black Wednesday when Britain had to quit the European Exchange Rate System.

图 8 "击败英格兰银行的人"——乔治·索罗斯

(Figure 8　George Soros, the Person Who Defeated the Bank of England)

1.7 现代金融理论大爆炸（Big Bang of Modern Financial Theory）

对于"宇宙大爆炸"理论，大家可能都听说过。在金融领域，同样经历过现代金融理论的大爆炸，时间大致在 1952 年到 1973 年。这二十年时间可谓现代金融理论的"黄金时代"——金融学家群星璀璨，各家理论令人眼花缭乱，一方面加深了人们对于金融本质的认识，另一方面也在以华尔街为主要战场的国际金融市场上不断掀起波澜。

Everyone may hear of the Big Bang Theory and in financial field, there also experienced big bang of modern financial theory roughly from 1952 to 1973. The twenty years may be called "the Golden Age" of modern financial theory when many financial economists appeared and all kinds of theories were dazzling. On the one hand, it made people deepen the cognition of essence of finance; on the other hand, great waves were raised constantly on international financial markets among which Wall Street was the main battle field.

我们先来看一串名单：

Let's first have a look at the following list：

1952 年，马科维茨资产组合理论。

In 1952, Makowitz created Portfolio Selection Theory.

1958 年,米勒和莫迪格利亚尼提出了著名的 MM 定理,即企业的市场价值与资本结构无关。

In 1958,Miller and Modigliani put forward the famous MM Theory, namely, the market value of enterprises has nothing to do with capital structure.

1976 年,斯蒂芬·罗斯提出套利定价理论。

In 1976,Stephen Ross put forward Arbitrage Pricing Theory(APT).

1964 年和 1965 年,夏普、林特勒和莫林提出资本资产定价理论。

In 1964 and 1965,Sharp, Lintner and Moline(S-L-M) put forward Capital Asset Pricing Model(CAPM).

1973 年,布莱克和斯科尔斯提出了 B-S 期权定价理论:创造和繁荣了金融衍生品市场。

In 1973,Black and Scholes put forward B-S Option Pricing Theory which created and boomed the financial derivative market.

那么他们提出的这些理论到底有什么内涵?对现代金融发展的实际又有什么意义?我们再来看一份名单:历年获得诺贝尔经济学奖的金融学家及其获奖理由。在经济学领域,这些巨匠们所取得的成绩恐怕没有比这个奖项的获奖理由更权威的解释了。

Then,what is the connotation of their theories? What is the significance of the theories for the modern financial development? Let's look at the other list——the financial economists who won the Nobel Economics Prize over the years and the reasons for awards. The achievements of these great masters are more than the more authoritative explanation for their awards in the field of economy.

表 1　历年获得诺贝尔经济学奖的金融学家及其主要贡献

年份	获奖者	获奖理由
1990	哈里·马科维茨(美国)	在金融经济学方面做出了开创性工作
	默顿·米勒(美国)	
	威廉·夏普（美国）	

续　表

年份	获奖者	获奖理由
1997	罗伯特·默顿（美国）	对布莱克-斯科尔斯公式所依赖的假设条件做了进一步减弱，在许多方面对其做了推广
	迈伦·斯科尔斯（美国）	给出了著名的布莱克—斯科尔斯期权定价公式，该法则已成为金融机构设计金融新产品的思想方法
2013	尤金·法玛（美国）	对资产价格的实证分析
	拉尔斯·彼得·汉森（美国）	
	罗伯特·希勒（美国）	

Table 1　Financial Economists Won the Nobel Economics Prize Over the Years and Their Chief Contributions

Year	Winner	Award Reason
1990	Harry Markowitz（U.S.A）	Contribution to the creativity of financial economics
	Merton Miller（U.S.A）	
	William Sharpe（U.S.A）	
1997	Robert Merton（U.S.A）	Futher weakening the assumed conditions depended on by Black - Scholes Formula and popularized it in many ways
	Myron Scholes（U.S.A）	Putting forward the famous B-S Option Pricing Formula which has become the method of thinking when financial institutions design new financial products
2013	Eugene Fama（U.S.A）	Making empirical analysis on assets price
	Peter Hansen（U.S.A）	
	Robert Shiller（U.S.A）	

　　作为金融长廊，我们不妨把他们的理论当作"艺术品"来欣赏：谁能三言两语把凡·高或者毕加索的作品说得清清楚楚呢？

　　As it is financial gallery, we may as well appreciate their theories as works of art—who can explain clearly in a few words about the works of Vincent Van Gogh and Picasso?

不过金融毕竟不同于艺术,因为它形式上的数学化让它的逻辑看上去严密得多,科学得多。如果非要用自然语言加以说明的话,那么现代金融理论的核心就是探讨在存在时间价值和风险(不确定性)的基础上,各种金融资产如何合理定价。在此基础之上,衍生出两个核心问题:一是公司如何运用各种金融资产工具,使资产结构最优化(即公司金融);二是各类投资主体如何获得最佳受益(即投资学)。

But finance is after all different to art because finance seems more exact and scientific in logic due to its mathematicization in form. If it must be stated in natural language, the core of modern financial theory is to probe how to reasonably price different financial assets on a basis of existing time value and risks (uncertainties). Two core problems were derived from the basis, one is how can the company make use of different financial asset tools to optimize asset structure (that is corporate finance); the other is how can different investors gain the best benefits (that is the Theory of Investment).

现代金融理论的基础假设是,金融市场是有效的,所以不存在免费的午餐(无风险套利机会),但是实际情况是,金融实践家和华尔街的精英们使出浑身解数,运用各种复杂的金融工具,根本目的就是要找到市场运行中的漏洞或者不完善之处,找到无风险套利的机会从而获取超额利润。

The foundational assumption of modern financial theory is that the market is effective and there is no free lunch (riskless arbitrage chances). But in fact, financial practitioners and elites on Wall Street try their very best and apply all kinds of complicated financial instruments with a primary purpose to seek out the loopholes or imperfections in the market operation as well as the riskless arbitrage chances to obtain super profits.

金融理论大爆炸的影响难以估量,随后金融发展可谓突飞猛进,一日千里。不过,这些威力巨大的金融"炸弹"用得不好,破坏力也是十分惊人的!

The influence of Big Bang of Financial Theory is immeasurable thereafter finance developed by leaps and bounds. However, the collapsing force is also striking if the powerful financial "bombs" are misused.

仅举两个例子,一是长期资本管理公司的破产,二是2008年开始席卷全球的金融海啸。

We take two examples: one is the bankruptcy of Long-Term Capital Management (LTCM) and the other is the financial tsunami which had swept the globe since 2008.

　　长期资本管理公司是美国华尔街首屈一指的对冲基金公司,其合伙人队伍可谓阵容豪华,包括凭借期权定价获得1997年诺贝尔经济学奖的罗伯特·默顿和迈伦·斯科尔斯,以及前美国财政部副部长兼美联储副主席戴维·马林斯。该公司成立于1994年,却在1998年年末就破产了。它在这五年间创造了对冲基金盈利的多项记录。1998年年初时其净资产达46亿美元,掌握的资产总额多达1500亿美元,财政杠杆比率为1∶33。公司主要合伙人个人资产都在亿万元以上。

LTCM was an American top hedge fund management firm whose partner troops are of high-level including Robert Merton and Myron Scholes (the Nobel Economics Prize winners in 1997 for their Option Pricing Theory) and David Mullins (the former vice-minister of Treasury Department of United States and vice-chairman of the FED). It was set up in 1994 and went broke at the end of 1998. It created a number of records of hedge fund profits in its five years. At the beginning of 1998, the corporation had a net asset of 4.6 billion dollars, and the total assets managed by it were up to 150 billion dollars with a leverage ratio of 1:33. The personal assets of its main partners were up to hundreds of millions dollars.

　　长期资本管理公司主要征战在股票套利、互换利率交易、股票波动率交易及全球市场套利等市场上,获利颇丰,但随后俄罗斯金融风暴引发了全球的金融动荡,长期资本管理公司一天的亏损就高达5.53亿美元。仅仅几周时间,长期资本管理公司就面临了1万亿美元的违约风险,最后难逃破产倒闭的命运。

LTCM mainly went on an expedition in the markets such as stock arbitrage, interest swap transaction, stock volatility transaction and global market arbitrage and made big profits from them. With the following Russian financial crisis triggering the global financial turbulence, LTCM lost 553 million dollars within a day. Only a few weeks, LTCM was confronted with one trillion dollars default risk and was eventually saddled with huge debts and pushed into bankruptcy.

图 9　在 2008 年金融海啸中破产的雷曼兄弟公司①

(Figure 9　Lehman Brothers Went Bankrupt in the Financial Tsunami in 2008)

　　2008 年金融海啸同样是一场"过度自信"导致"过度投机"而引发的经济灾难。这次金融海啸的导火索是 2007 年浮现的次贷危机。在宽松的货币政策下,从 20 世纪末开始,美国的次级贷款②数量大增,但是华尔街精英们通过复杂的金融工程技术,把这些先天质地不良的贷款重新分割、组合,包装成各种收益较高,又看上去比较安全的证券,吸引包括大型商业银行、保险公司在内的各类机构投资者购买。但是,这些高收益、低风险的投资品的底座并不坚实,因为这座大厦是建立在房价始终上涨的前提之上的。一旦房价出现逆转,次贷违约率就会上升,这座建在沙滩上的大厦就会轰然倒塌。

　　The financial tsunami in 2008 was also an economic disaster triggered by overspeculation because of overconfidence. Subprime crisis emerged in 2007 was its blasting fuse. Since the end of the 20th century, American subprime lending had increased rapidly due to the easy monetary policy. The elites on Wall Street split and combined those congenitally bad loans again and packed them into higher earnings and seemly safer securities by means of complicated financial engineering technology in order to attract different types of institutional investors including large-scale commercial banks and insurance companies to buy. Nevertheless, these investment products seemed to be of high-profit and low-risk were not solid in foundation because the mansion was established on the basis of the assumption that the housing price would always rise. Once the price started to reverse, the default rate of subprime lending would increase, and the

---

　　①　雷曼兄弟公司成立于 1850 年,破产前是美国第四大投行,曾经在华尔街叱咤风云,风光无限。

　　②　次级贷款是指一些贷款机构向信用程度较差和收入不高的借款人提供的贷款。因借贷者的偿还能力较低,次级贷款的违约风险较高。

mansion which was built up on sand beach would collapse at once.

次贷危机爆发后，投资者开始对按揭证券的价值失去信心，由此引发了流动性危机。虽然多国中央银行多次向金融市场注入巨额资金，但仍没有阻止这场金融危机的爆发。直到 2008 年 9 月，这场金融危机开始失控，并导致多间相当大型的金融机构倒闭或被政府接管，并引发经济衰退。至今，不少深受金融海啸之苦的国家仍然在经济复苏的道路上艰难前行。

After the subprime crisis, investors began to lose confidence in the value of mortgage-backed securities, which led to the liquidity crisis. Even though many central banks injected huge sum of funds into the financial markets many times, the explosion of monetary crisis could not be held back. The financial crisis started to be out of control till September, 2008, which resulted in the close-down of considerable large-scale financial institutions or the take-over by the government and consequently triggered the economic recession. So far, not a few countries suffered from the financial tsunami have been proceding with hardship on the way to economic recovery.

好了，我们的漫步金融长廊也即将告一段落。在结束这段愉快的旅程之前，我们不妨再来回顾一下刚刚看过的风景。

Well, the wandering along the financial gallery is coming to a conclusion. Before we stop the pleasant journey, let's look back to the sights we have just enjoyed.

金融最通俗的含义就是资金的流通，资金流通最初和基本的手段和工具是货币，但是金融的本质是信用和清算体系。信用有两个重要维度：时间价值和风险管理，可以说一切现代的金融工具、金融市场和金融机构都是围绕它们展开的。在现代经济社会，金融要能够有效、安全地运作，一方面离不开金融理论的深入探索，另一方面在实际层面需要构建和完善金融制度。

The most popular meaning of finance is the circulation of capital, the original and essential means and tools of which is currency, but the nature of finance are credit and clearing systems. Credit has two important dimensions of time value and risk management around which all modern financial instruments, financial markets and financial institutions are working. In the modern economic society, finance cannot operate effectively and safely without thorough research on financial theories and the construction and perfection of financial systems in practice.

　　如果你还意犹未尽，那么，可以继续阅读本书的后续章节和专题，或者追踪参考书目的书刊资料进一步阅读，或者运用搜索引擎到网上冲浪，或者找专业领域的老师、朋友聊一聊……

　　If you are wanting more, you may continue to read the following chapters and subjects, trace the reference books for a further reading, surf the internet by means of the search engines, or discuss with the specialized teachers and friends...

　　希望了解金融知识、运用金融知识能够让你的生活更美好。

　　We sincerely hope that your life will be more beautiful by understanding finance knowledge and making the best use of it.

2 货币史话
（Money Myth）

2.0 导言（Introduction）

　　货币是指从商品中分离出来的固定充当一般等价物的商品。历史上充当一般等价物的商品有很多,如牲畜、布匹、贝壳等。后来,贵金属金银由于具有体积小、价值大、易于分割、不易磨损、便于保存和携带等特点,逐步从商品中分离出来而固定地充当了一般等价物。在我国历史的漫漫长河中,货币经历了实物货币、金属货币、信用货币和电子货币等不同的阶段。

　　Money, separated from other commodities, is the special commodity legally acting as universal equivalent. There were many kinds of commodities that acted as general equivalents in the history such as domestic animals, cloth, shells, etc. Afterwards, precious metals such as gold and silver gradually separated from other commodities to be the universal equivalents due to its many features of being in small size, great value, easy to split, difficult to wear, easy to store and carry. In the long history of our country, money has gone through different stages from commodity money to metallic money, then to credit money and electronic money, etc.

2.1 实物货币(Commodity Money)

实物货币是具有价值和使用价值,但价值较低,价格容易波动,不易贮藏或携带的货币。贝壳、羽毛、珊瑚、布帛、活牲畜、烟草、可可豆等都充当过货币。

Commodity money is a kind of money that has value and value in use, but its value is a little bit low and price is rather volatile, and it is difficult to deposit or carry around. Shells, feathers, corals, cloth and silk, livestock, tobacco and cocoa beans all played the role of money in the history.

贝币(Money Cowrie)

在人类早期的经济活动中,一种名为货贝的贝壳,以其坚固耐磨、光洁美丽、易于携带和具有自然单位的特点,充当了商品交换的媒介,这即是最原始的货币。

In early economic activities of human beings, a kind of shells named cowrie shells acted as the medium of goods exchange because of its features of being sturdy and resistant to wear, bright and clean, easy to carry and having natural unit. This was also the primitive money in the history.

在货币史上,用贝壳当货币流通时间较长,使用范围也较广。世界上许多民族都有用贝壳充当货币的历史。在古代亚洲,除中国用贝壳外,今日之印度、斯里兰卡、孟加拉国等,都有使用贝壳的历史;在美洲,当西方殖民者在 16 世纪首次踏上这个大陆的时候,他们发现当地的印第安人使用的货币就是贝壳;在非洲,一直到 20 世纪初,包括坦桑尼亚、埃塞俄比亚等国在内的绝大多数部落依然在使用贝壳作为货币。

In the history of money, cowrie shells were long and widely used as money in circulation. There are many nationalities in the world that have the history of using cowrie shells as money. In ancient Asia, besides China, today's India, Sri Lanka, Bangladesh, also once used shells for payment. In America, Western colonialists, who first set foot on the large continent in the 16th century, found that the local Indians used shells as their money. In Africa, most tribes in countries including Tanzania and Ethiopia used shells as their money till the early 20th century.

2.2 金属货币 (Metallic Money)

金属货币价值大,体积小,便于携带,易于保存。中国是世界上最早以铜铸币的国家,公元前 1500 年,商代已有铜贝币。公元前 800 年,春秋初期已有青铜铸造的布币和刀币。

Metallic money is a kind of money that has high value but small volume, easy to carry and deposit. China was the first country to mint coins from copper. In 1500 B. C., in the Shang Dynasty, there existed copper money cowrie. In 800 B. C., in the early Spring and Autumn Period, spade-shaped coin and knife money made of bronze were used in trading.

布币 (Spade-shaped Coin)

布币是中国古代货币,因形状似铲,又称铲布。布币是春秋战国时期流通于中原诸国的铲状铜币。铲状工具曾是民间交易的媒介,故最早出现的铸币铸成了铲状。

Spade-shaped coin was ancient money in China, and was also named spade cloth because its shape was just like a spade. This kind of money was circulated in the central plains during the Spring and Autumn Period in China. The tools in the shape of spade were once a medium of exchange among the people, so the firstly-appeared minted coins were in the shape of spade.

刀币 (Knife Money)

刀币因其形状像刀而得名。刀币是一种中国古代的铜币名,由刀这一生产工具演变而成。刀币也是对春秋战国时期铸行的针首刀、尖首刀和圆首刀等各种刀形货币的总称。流通于春秋战国时期的齐、燕、赵等国,上面铸有文字。秦始皇统一中国后,统一币制,废贝币、刀币、布币等。其后,王莽所铸造的钱币中有金错刀。

Knife money became well-known for it was in a shape of knife. It was one of the ancient copper coins in China which was derived from the tool-knife. Knife money was the general term for the money in the shape such as needle-knife, sharp-knife and circular-knife during the Spring and Autumn Period and circulated in Qi, Yan and Zhao, etc. On the knives, there were casted characters. After Qin Shi Huang (the First Emperor of China) unified China and money, shell money, knife money and cloth money were abandoned. Thereafter, Wang Mang minted the coins including Gold Cuo Knife.

2.3 信用货币（Credit Money）

信用货币不具有价值和使用价值，凭借信用和政府强制流通，主要包括银行券和纸币。信用货币贮藏和携带方便，数量可进行调节，能够满足经济发展和商品交换的需求。

Credit money, including bank notes and paper money, has no value nor value in use, and is forced to circulate by the credit and government. It is very easy to deposit and carry, and with an adjustable amount to meet the requirements of economic development and commodity exchanges.

2.4 电子货币（Electronic Money）

电子货币也称虚拟货币，是纸币、硬币和现金的电子等价物，也是金融电子化、信息化的产物。电子货币的铸造成本极低，具体形态多样化，交易、贮藏及携带极为方便，能够极好地满足经济发展和商品交换的需求。

Electronic money also named virtual currency, refers to the electronic equivalent which was the historical result of financial computerization and informationalization. Electronic money bears low cost and diverse shapes. It is also very easy to trade, deposit and carry, and meets the demand for the economic development and goods exchange well.

信用卡（Credit Card）

信用卡是银行向个人和单位发行的，凭此向特约单位消费和向银行存取现金，具有消费信用的特制载体卡片。其形式是一张正面印有发卡银行名称、有效期、号码、持卡人姓名等内容，背面有磁条、签名条的卡片。

Credit card is special carrier card with consumer credit issued by banks to individuals and institutions, whereby it's allowed to consume and save or draw cash to special units. It is in the form of a card with the name of the issuing bank, the expiration date, the number, and the card holder on the front, and with magnetic strip and signature strip on the back.

2.5 货币职能（Function of Money）

货币的职能——钱是干什么用的？

Function of money—what is money used for?

经济学中的货币，狭义地讲，是用作交换商品的标准物品；广义地讲，是充当交换媒介、价值尺度、价值贮藏和支付手段的物品。具体地讲，货币具有交换媒介、价值标准、延期支付标准、价值贮藏、世界货币等职能。

Money in economics refers to the standard commodity used to exchange for another commodity in a narrow sense; it is the commodity used as medium of exchange, measure of value, store of value and means of payment in a broad sense. Specifically, the main functions of money are distinguished as: medium of exchange, measure of value, standard of deferred payment, store of value and world currency.

交换媒介（Medium of Exchange）

交换媒介又称"交易媒介""交易手段"，指用于购买商品或服务的媒介工具。货币可充当交换媒介，货币的这种职能被称为"流通手段"。

Medium of exchange, also known as medium of trade or means of trade, refers to the medium used to purchase goods or services. Money can act as a medium of exchange. This function of money is called means of circulation.

价值尺度（Measure of Value）

价值尺度是用来衡量和表现商品价值的一种职能，是货币最基本、最重要的职能。正如衡量长度的尺子本身有长度，称东西的砝码本身有重量一样，衡量商品价值的货币本身也是商品，具有价值；没有价值的东西，不能充当价值尺度。

When the value of goods is frequently used to measure and compare the value of other goods or where its value is used to denominate debts, it is functioning as measure of value. Those that have no value can't be used as measure of value. Measure of value is the most basic and important function of money. The money also is ammodity in itself when measuring the value of other goods.

价值贮藏（Store of Value）

货币作为贮藏手段，是随着商品生产和商品流通的发展而不断发展的。在商品流通的初期,有些人就把多余的产品换成货币保存起来,贮藏金银被看作富裕的表现,这是一种朴素的货币贮藏形式。随着商品生产的连续进行,商品生产者要不断地买进生产资料和生活资料,但他生产和出卖自己的商品要花费时间,并且对能否卖掉也没有把握。这样,为了能够不断地买进,他就必须把前次出卖商品所得的货币贮藏起来,这是商品生产者的货币贮藏。随着商品流通的扩展,货币的权力日益增大,很多东西都可以用货币来买卖,货币交换扩展到众多领域。

Money is used as means of store and it is purchased primarily to store value for future trade. This function results from the belief or trust that the form of money will retain value over time. At the primary stage of commodity circulation, some people would change the excessive products to money and then deposited them, thus storing up gold and silver was considered being rich, which was also the plain form of depositing money. With the successive production of products, the manufacturers had to continuously buy means of production and livelihood, whereas it took them some time to produce and sell their productions which was not very sure for them. Therefore, the manufacturer had to sell the commodities he had produced and stored the money up before he could buy the raw and processed materials again, which was the hoard of money of commodity producers. With the extension of the commodity circulation, the power of money was increasing accordingly, many things can be bought with money and the exchange of money was extended to various fields.

支付手段(Means of Payment)

货币作为独立的价值形式进行单方面运动(如清偿债务、缴纳税款、支付工资和租金等)时所执行的职能。货币作为支付手段的职能是适应商品生产和商品交换发展的需要而产生的。

Means of payment is a function of money when it is used to repay the debts, pay the taxes, salaries and rents, etc., in an independent form of value. This function is the result to meet the demands for good production and exchange.

2.6 "币"海拾遗 (Stories Behind Currencies)

人民币史话 (The History of RMB)

1948年12月1日,中国人民银行成立。人民币的发行至今已有近70年的历史,至目前为止,中国人民银行已先后发行了五套人民币。

On December 1, 1948, the People's Bank of China was set up and meanwhile started to issue RMB. It has been almost seventy years of the issuance of RMB and up to now, there has been five sets of RMB successively in the history.

人民币的全称是中华人民共和国货币,是中华人民共和国的法定货币。根据国际标准组织 ISO 4217 的规定,其正式的国际货币代码为 CNY,不过国际上更习惯的缩写形式是 RMB;在数字前一般加上"¥"表示人民币的金额。1948年12月1日中国人民银行成立时,开始发行第一套人民币;1955年3月1日开始发行第二套人民币;1962年4月15日开始发行第三套人民币;1987年4月27日开始发行第四套人民币。目前市场上流通的人民币以第五套为主,还有部分第四套人民币。人民币的单位为元(圆)(人民币元,简写为"RMB",以"¥"为代号)。人民币辅币单位为角、分。人民币没有规定法定含金量,它和其他货币一样,执行价值尺度、流通手段、支付手段等职能。

RMB (short for Renminbi Yuan) is the legal currency in the People's Republic of China with the three-letter currency codes "CNY" (Chinese Yuan) defined in ISO 4217, but more habitually abbreviated as RMB internationally. The symbol of "¥" is added in front of the figures to show the definite amount. The first set of Renminbi Yuan was released on December 1, 1948 when the People's Bank of China was set up, and the second set issued on March 1, 1955; the third on April 15, 1962 and the fourth on April 27, 1987. The fifth set includes the notes mainly in current circulation, still with part of the fourth set. The unit of RMB is Yuan, or Renminbi Yuan with the abbreviation of RMB and the mark "¥". The fractional coins of RMB include Jiao and Fen. Like other currencies, RMB carries out the functions as common measure of value, means of circulation and means of payment, etc., though there is no legally prescribed gold content in it.

在中国,中国人民银行是国家管理人民币的主管机关,负责人民币的设计、印制和发行。人民币的单位为元,人民币的辅币单位为角、分。1元等于10角,1角等于10分。除1、2、5分三种硬币外,第一套、第二套和第三套人民币已经退出流通,目前流通的人民币,是中国人民银行自1987年以来发行的第四套人民币和1999年陆续发行的第五套人民币,两套人民币同时流通。

In China, the People's Bank of China, national administration of Renminbi, is responsible for the design, printing and issuance of the currency. The unit of RMB is Yuan, and the fractional coins are Jiao and Fen. One Yuan equals ten Jiao and one Jiao is ten Fen. Nowadays, the first three sets of RMB have been retreated from circulation except the coins of One Fen, Two Fen and Five Fen. The currencies we use now are the fourth set in 1987 and the fifth one in 1999.

第一套人民币(The First Set of RMB)

1948年12月1日,中国人民银行成立并发行第一套人民币,共12种面额,62种版别,其中1元券2种、5元券4种、10元券4种、20元券7种、50元券7种、100元券10种、200元券5种、500元券6种、1000元券6种、5000元券5种、10000元券4种、50000元券2种。

On the first day of December in 1948, the People's Bank of China was set up and the first set of RMB was released, with 12 denominations and 62 versions, among which One Yuan has two versions, Five Yuan four versions, Ten Yuan four versions, Twenty Yuan seven versions, Fifty Yuan seven versions, One Hundred Yuan ten versions, Two Hundred Yuan five versions, Five Hundred Yuan six versions, One Thousand Yuan six versions, Five Thousand Yuan five versions, Ten Thousand Yuan four versions and Fifty Thousand Yuan two versions.

统一发行人民币结束了几十年通货膨胀的局面和中国近百年外币、金银币在市场流通买卖的历史,促进了人民解放战争的全面胜利,在中华人民共和国成立初期经济恢复时期发挥了重要作用。

Issuing RMB finalized the inflation for several decades and the history of buying and selling of foreign currencies, gold and silver coins in circulation market for about one hundred years. The universal issuance of RMB also promoted the overall victory of the Chinese People's War of Liberation and played an important role in the recovery period of economy in the early years of the establishment of the People's Republic of China.

图 1　第一套人民币样张

(Figure 1　The Sample of the First Set of RMB)

第二套人民币 (The Second Set of RMB)

第二套人民币于 1955 年 3 月 1 日开始发行,同时收回第一套人民币。第二套人民币和第一套人民币折合比率为 1∶10000。第二套人民币共有 1 分、2 分、5 分、1 角、2 角、5 角、1 元、2 元、3 元、5 元、10 元 11 个面额,其中 1 元券有 2 种,5 元券有 2 种,1 分、2 分和 5 分券别有纸币、硬币 2 种。为便于流通,自 1957 年 12 月 1 日起发行 1 分、2 分、5 分三种硬币,与纸币等值流通。1961 年 3 月 25 日和 1962 年 4 月 20 日分别发行了黑色 1 元券和棕色 5 元券,分别对票面图案、花纹进行了调整和更换。由于大面额钞票技术要求很高,在当时情况下,3 元、5 元、10 元由苏联代印。

The second set of RMB started to be released on March 1, 1955 when the first set was withdrawn. The exchange rate between the second set and the first set was one to ten thousand. The second set was composed of 11 denominations such as One Fen, Two Fen, Five Fen, One Jiao, Two Jiao, Five Jiao, One Yuan, Two Yuan, Three Yuan, Five Yuan and Ten Yuan, among which One Yuan and Five Yuan had two versions respectively, and One Fen, Two Fen as well as Five Fen had two versions both in notes and coins. In order to be convenient for circulation, the coins with denominations of One Fen, Two Fen and Five Fen released from 1957 were in equivalent with their note versions. The black One Yuan paper notes and brown Five Yuan notes were released respectively on March 25, 1961 and April 20, 1962, whose facial design and patterns were also adjusted and changed. Owing to the high technical requirements for large denominations, the notes of Three Yuan, Five Yuan and Ten Yuan were printed by the Soviet Union (disintegrated in 1991) instead.

第二套人民币设计主题思想明确,印制工艺技术先进,主辅币结构合理,图案颜色新颖。主景图案集中体现了中国社会主义建设的风貌,表现了中国共产党革命的战斗历程和各族人民大团结的主题思想。在印制工艺上除了分币外,其他券别全部采用胶凹套印,凹印版是以我国传统的手工雕刻方法制作的,具有独特的民族风格,其优点是版纹深、墨层厚,有较好的反假防伪功能。

The second set of RMB had clear design theme, reasonable standard and fractional structure, and novel pattern and color, using advanced printing technology. The main pattern embodied the construction of Chinese socialism, performed the struggle course of Chinese communist revolution and the unity theme of people of all ethnic groups. In the printing process except cents, other coupons used gravure method. This version was made by Chinese traditional hand carving, and had a unique national style, with the advantages of deep schlieren, thick ink layer and good anti fake security function.

图 2　第二套人民币样张
(Figure 2　The Sample of the Second Set of RMB)

第三套人民币(The Third Set of RMB)

第三套人民币于 1962 年 4 月 15 日发行,共有 1 角、2 角、5 角、1 元、2 元、5 元、10 元 7 种面额、13 种版别,其中 1 角券别有 4 种(包括 1 种硬币),2 角、5 角、1 元有纸币、硬币 2 种。1966 年和 1967 年,又先后两次对 1 角纸币进行改版,主要是增加满版水印,调整背面颜色。

The third set of RMB started to be released on April 15, 1962, including seven denominations and thirteen versions of One Jiao, Two Jiao, Five Jiao,

One Yuan，Two Yuan，Five Yuan and Ten Yuan，among which One Jiao had four versions（a coin version included），Two Jiao，Five Jiao，One Yuan were both in the form of notes and coins. The notes of One Jiao were revised twice in 1966 and 1967 mainly by adding watermark full page and adjusting the color of the riverside of the notes.

第三套人民币票面设计图案比较集中地反映了当时中国国民经济以农业为基础、以工业为主导、农轻重并举的方针。在印制工艺上，第三套人民币继承和发扬了第二套人民币的技术传统、风格。制版过程中，精雕细刻，机器和传统的手工相结合，使图案、花纹线条精细；油墨配色合理，色彩新颖、明快；票面纸幅较小，图案美观大方。

The facial design of the third set intensively mirrored national economy at that time with the features of agriculture-based，industry-oriented with agriculture，light and heavy industry to be developed simultaneously. The printed technology of the third set inherited and carried forward the traditional technique and style in refined carving and the combination of machine and handwork which made the pattern，figure and line more meticulous，the ink and color blending more reasonable，the color more original and much brighter. The size of the banknotes is smaller but with an elegant appearance.

这套人民币是世界上最有社会主义特色和创新意识的货币，主题画面紧扣生产力的提高，科技元素丰富。这套人民币发行时，货币发行与物资分配严格由中央综合平衡，全面安排。我国人民币货币一元化，巩固独立自主、长期稳定的货币，成为世界上少有的稳定货币。

This set of RMB is the most creative currency of typical features of socialism in the world with a theme sticking to the improvement of productivity as well as rich elements of science and technology. This set of currency was issued the issuance of currency and allocation of materials should be strictly balanced and arranged by the central government. Unified currency was the principle at that time to consolidate the independent and stable currency and become the rare steady currency in the world.

图 3　第三套人民币样张

(Figure 3　The Sample of the Third Set of RMB)

第四套人民币（The Fourth Set of RMB）

为了适应经济发展的需要，进一步健全中国的货币制度，方便流通使用和交易核算，中国人民银行自 1987 年 4 月 27 日起，开始发行第四套人民币。共有 1 角、2 角、5 角、1 元、2 元、5 元、10 元、50 元和 100 元 9 种面额，其中 1 角、5 角、1 元有纸币、硬币 2 种。与第三套人民币相比，增加了 50 元、100 元大面额人民币。为适应反假人民币工作需要，1992 年 8 月 20 日，中国人民银行又发行了改版后的 1990 年版 50 元、100 元券，增加了安全线。

To meet the demands of economic development，further perfect China's monetary policy and facilitate the circulation，use and transactions，the People's Bank of China released the fourth set of RMB on April 27，1987，including nine denominations of One Jiao，Two Jiao，Five Jiao，One Yuan，Two Yuan，Five Yuan，Ten Yuan，Fifty Yuan and One Hundred Yuan，among which One Jiao，Five Jiao and One Yuan had two versions both in notes and coins. Large denominations in Fifty Yuan and One Hundred Yuan were added compared with the third set. In order to meet the demand for anti-counterfeit notes，the revised Fifty Yuan and One Hundred Yuan notes of 1990 version were released from August 20，1992 with increased security thread.

第四套人民币在设计思想、风格和印制工艺上都有一定的创新和突破。主景图案集中体现了在中国共产党领导下，中国各族人民意气风发，团结一致，建设中国特色社会主义的主题思想。在设计风格上，这套人民币保持和发扬了中华民族艺术传统特点，主币背面图景取材于中国名胜古迹、名山大川，背面纹饰全部采用富有中华民族特点的图案。在印制工艺上，主景全部采用了大幅人物头像水印，雕刻工艺复杂;钞票纸分别采用了满版水印和固定人像水印,它不仅表现出线条图景,而且表现出明暗层次,工艺技术很高,进一步提高了中国印钞工艺技术水平和钞票防伪能力。

The fourth set of RMB had innovations and breakthrough in the design idea, style and the printing technology. The main design of this set fully represented the theme of people of all nationalities in China united firmly to construct the socialism with Chinese characteristics with high spirit and vigor under the leadership of the Communist Party of China (CPC). It maintained and carried forward the traditional features of China's national art in terms of design style. The reverse side of the unit currency drew materials of national scenic spots and historic sites as well as the well-known mountains and rivers, while the ornamentation of the back side employed the graphic patterns full of national characteristics. When it comes to the printing technology, the main features of the fourth set all employed the watermark of big head portrait with complicated artistic carving. The notes adopted full watermark and fixed figure watermark to manifest not only the line prospect but also the shade of grey with high technique which improved Chinese banknote printing technology and the anti-counterfeit ability.

图 4　第四套人民币样张

(Figure 4　The Sample of the Fourth Set of RMB)

第五套人民币(The Fifth Set of RMB)

1999 年 10 月 1 日起,中国人民银行陆续发行第五套人民币,共有 1 角、5 角、1 元、5 元、10 元、20 元、50 元、100 元 8 种面额,其中 1 角、5 角、1 元有纸币、硬币 2 种。第五套人民币根据市场流通需要,增加了 20 元面额,取消了 2 元面额,使面额结构更加合理。

The People's Bank of China released the fifth set of RMB successively on October 1, 1999, including eight denominations of One Jiao, Five Jiao, One Yuan, Five Yuan, Ten Yuan, Twenty Yuan, Fifty Yuan and One Hundred Yuan, among which the denominations of One Jiao, Five Jiao and One Yuan had two versions of notes and coins. The Twenty Yuan denomination was added and the Two Yuan was abolished in the fifth set to meet the needs of market circulation and make the structures of denomination more reasonable.

第五套人民币继承了中国印制技术的传统经验,借鉴了国外钞票设计的先进技术,在防伪性能和适应货币处理现代化方面有了较大提高。各面额货币正面均采用毛泽东主席在中华人民共和国成立初期时的头像,底衬采用了中国著名花卉图案,背面主景图案通过选用有代表性的寓有民族特色的图案,充分表现了中国悠久的历史和壮丽的山河,弘扬了中国伟大的民族文化。

The printing technique of the fifth set inherited the traditional experience of Chinese graphic technology and used the experience in currency design of other countries for reference, thus improving the abilities of anti-fake nature and the modernized disposal of currencies. The obverse sides of different denominations employ the head portrait of Mao Zedong, first chairman of the People's Republic of China, with the bottom liners of Chinese famous ramages. The main designs of reverse sides are typical patterns bearing the national features which fully demonstrate the long history and splendid land of China, and carry forward the great national culture.

图 5　第五套人民币样张
(Figure 5　The Sample of the Fifth Set of RMB)

美元的历史（The History of United States Dollars，USD）

美元，又称美圆、美金，是美国的官方货币。它的出现与 1792 年美国《铸币法案》有关。它同时也作为储备货币在美国以外的国家广泛使用。当前美元的发行由美国联邦储备系统控制。最常用的表示美元的符号是"＄"，而用来表示美分的标志是"¢"。国际标准化组织为美元取的 ISO 4217 标准代号为 USD。美元纸币正面主景图案为人物头像，主色调为黑色。背面主景图案为建筑，主色调为绿色，但不同版别的颜色稍有差异，如 1934 年版背面为深绿色，1950 年版背面为草绿色，1963 年版背面为墨绿色。在美国发行的各种美元币种中，联邦储备券系列包括 500、1000、5000、10000 美元面值，金币券包括 1000、10000 和 100000 美元面值。其他币种没有面额超过 100 美元的大额纸币。

United States Dollars(USD)，also called American Dollars，is the official currency in the United States of America. The birth of United States Dollars was due to the *Coinage Act* passed by the Congress in 1792. Now it is also widely used as reserve currency in other countries. The release of US Dollars is currently controlled by the Federal Reserve System. The most common symbol of dollar is "＄" while "¢" for cents. USD is the standard code for US Dollars according to ISO 4217. The design of the right side of dollar notes is figures with the main color in black. The design of the reverse side is buildings in green with rare difference in color for different versions, for example, dark green for version in 1934 but grass green for that in 1950, black green for 1963. Among all the currencies issued in the United States, Federal Reserve notes include the denominations in 500, 1000, 5000 and 10000, gold certificates are in 1000, 10000 and 100000. Other currencies don't have bills in denominations larger than 100 US Dollars.

1933 年 3 月 9 日，美国总统罗斯福签署总统令，终止了金币券的流通，将其不论面额全部收回。至 1940 年，金币券回收完毕。1946 年以后，美国不再发行新的大面额纸币，至 1969 年，所有面额在 100 美元以上的大面额纸币全部退出流通。目前流通使用的美元是 1969 年后的版本。美元是世界上的基础外汇品种。

On March 9, 1933, President Roosevelt signed Presidential Proclamation to terminate the circulation of gold certificates and withdraw all of them in different denominations. The withdrawal was finished in 1940. The United

States no longer released paper notes with large denominations after 1946 and all notes larger than 100 US Dollars were retreated from circulation until 1969. Now the edition in use is released after 1969. The USD is the foundation money of foreign exchange currency.

1 美元券(1993)正面是首任美国总统乔治·华盛顿(1732—1799)肖像,背景主景是美国国玺。

The front side of the one-dollar note issued in 1993 is the portrait of George Washington (1732—1799), the first president of the United States of America, the reverse is the Great Seal of the United States.

(1美元正面 The Front Side of $1)　　　(1美元反面 The Reverse Side of $1)

2 美元券(1976)正面是第 3 任美国总统托马斯·杰斐逊(1743—1826)的肖像,为斯图亚特原作。背面是杰弗逊故居(1976 年以前版)、《独立宣言》签字会场(1976 年以后版)。

The front side of the two-dollar note issued in 1976 is the portrait of Thomas Jefferson (1743—1826), third president of the United States of America, the original work of G. C. Stuart. The reverse is the former residence of Jefferson (version before 1976) and signature council house of the *Declaration of Independence* (version after 1976).

(2美元正面 The Front Side of $2)　　　(2美元反面 The Reverse Side of $2)

5 美元券(1995、1999)正面是废除奴隶制的美国第 16 任总统亚伯拉罕·林肯(1809—1865)的肖像,背面是位于华盛顿的林肯纪念堂。

The front side of the five-dollar note (issued in 1995 and 1999) is the portrait of Abraham Lincoln (1809—1865), the sixteenth president who abolished the slavery of the United States. The reverse is Lincoln Memorial located in Washington.

(5美元正面 The Front Side of $5)　　(5美元反面 The Reverse Side of $5)

10 美元券（1999）正面是美国第一任财政部部长亚历山大·汉密尔顿（1755—1804）的肖像，背面是美国财政部大楼。

The front side of the ten-dollar note（issued in 1999）is the portrait of Alexander Hamilton（1755—1804），the first finance minister of the United States. The reverse is the building of Treasury Department of the United States.

(10美元正面 The Front Side of $10)　　(10美元反面 The Reverse Side of $10)

20 美元券（1995、1996、2004）正面是第 17 任美国总统安德鲁·杰克逊（1808—1875）的肖像，背面是美国总统府白宫。

The front side of the twenty-dollar note（issued in 1995，1996 and 2004）is the portrait of Andrew Jackson（1808—1875），the seventeenth president of the United States. The reverse is White House，office of the President.

50 美元券（1990、1996）正面是第 18 任总统尤利斯·格兰特（1822—1885）的肖像，背面是美国国会大厦。

The front side of the fifty-dollar note（issued in 1990 and 1996）is the portrait of Ulysses Simpson Grant（1822—1885），the eighteenth president of the United States. The reverse is United States Capitol.

100 美元券（1988、1996）正面不是总统，而是著名科学家、政治家、金融家本杰明·富兰克林（1706—1790）的肖像，他曾在美国独立战争时期起草著名的《独立宣言》。背面是费城独立纪念堂。

The front side of the one-hundred-dollar note（issued in 1988 and 1996）is the portrait of Benjamin Franklin（1706—1790），famous scientist，politician and financier instead of a president of the United States，who drafted the well-known *Declaration of Independence* during the Independent War. The reverse is the Memorial Hall of Independence in Philadelphia.

500 美元券正面是有"繁荣总统"之美名的美国第 25 任总统威廉·麦金莱 (1843—1901)的肖像,背面是面额小写"500"字饰,字体大小不一。

The front side of the five-hundred-dollar note is the portrait of William McKinley (1843—1901), the twenty-fifth president of the United States, who enjoyed the good reputation of "Prosperous President". The reverse is the figure of "500" in various body sizes.

1000 美元正面是第 22 和 24 任美国总统,唯一分开任两届的总统克利夫兰 (1827—1908)的肖像。背面是美国国名和大写"One Thousand"字饰。

The front side of the one-thousand-dollar note is the portrait of Cleveland (1827—1908), the twenty-second and twenty-fourth president of the United States, who was the only president being appointed for two periods respectively. The reverse is the name of the United States and the word of "One Thousand" in capital.

5000 美元正面是"美国宪法之父"、第四任总统麦迪逊(1751—1836)的肖像, 背面是面额小写"5000"字饰。

The front side of the five-thousand-dollar note is the portrait of Madison (1751—1836), the fourth president of the United States and "the Father of the Constitution". The reverse is the figure of "5000".

10000 美元正面是美国财政部部长萨蒙·蔡斯(1808—1873)的肖像,背面是 面额小写"10000"字饰。100000 美元金元券是美国财政部印刷局印制的最高面额 钞票,投入流通总量为 42000 张,仅在联邦储备银行内部用于官方转账。正面是美 国总统中"学术地位最高"的,被认为是美国历史上最杰出的六位总统之一的伍德 罗·威尔逊(1856—1924)的肖像,背面是半块金币等纹饰。

The front side of the ten-thousand-dollar note is the portrait of Salmon Portland Chase (1808—1873), the minister of the Treasury of the United States. The reverse is the figure of "10000". The one-hundred-thousand gold dollar note is the biggest denomination printed by the Printing Bureau of the Treasury of the United States with a total amount of 42000 in circulation only used within Feds for official transfer. The front side of the note is the portrait of Woodrow Wilson (1856—1924), one of the most outstanding six presidents in the history of the United States together with his highest academic position. The reverse is the ornamentation of half gold coin and so on.

英镑史话 (The History of Pound Sterling，GBP)

英镑是英国国家货币和货币单位名称。英镑主要由英格兰银行发行,但亦有其他发行机构。最常用于表示英镑的符号是"£"。国际标准化组织为英镑取的 ISO 4217 货币代码为 GBP。除了英国本土,英国海外领地的货币也以镑作为单位,与英镑的汇率固定为 1:1。英镑辅币单位原为先令和便士,1 英镑等于 10 先令,1 先令等于 10 便士。1971 年 2 月 15 日,英格兰银行实行新的货币进位制,辅币单位改为新便士,1 英镑等于 100 新便士。流通中的纸币有 5、10、20 和 50 面额的英镑,另有 1、2、5、10、20、50 新便士及 1 英镑的铸币。

Pound sterling is the national currency as well as the monetary unit of the United Kingdom. Pound is mainly issued by the Bank of England; it's also released by other issuing institutions. The most common symbol of pound is "£" and GBP (Great Britain Pound) as its currency code by ISO 4217. Besides, the overseas territories of Britain also employs Pound as their monetary unit with an exchange rate fixed at 1:1. In the past, the fractional currencies of pound are shilling and penny. One Pound is Ten Shillings and One Shilling is Ten Pennies. On February 15, 1971, the Bank of England implemented new currency scale and the fractional currency was changed into new penny by one pound being one hundred new pennies. The notes in circulation have denominations of five, ten, twenty and fifty in pounds and one, two, five, ten, twenty and fifty in new penny as well as one-pound coin.

英镑是英国官方货币,是目前历史最悠久的仍然被使用的货币。英镑占全球外汇储备的第三名,仅次于美元和欧元。英镑是第四大外汇交易币种,排在美元、欧元和日元之后。

As the British official currency, pound is the currency with the longest history among those still used currencies after the employment of Euro Dollars. It is the third foreign exchange reserve next to US Dollars and Euro Dollars. Pound is the fourth foreign exchange currency with a total amount next to US Dollars, Euro Dollars and Japanese Yen in the global market.

英镑可自由兑换成其他货币,也可以在全世界的外汇交易市场中被买卖。它的价值相对于其他货币是波动的,但历史上,英镑一直是最有价值的基础外汇品种。

Pound can be freely changed into other currencies and exchanged in the foreign exchange market. Though its value is fluctuant against other currencies, Pound is the most valuable foundation money of foreign exchange currency in the history.

欧元(Euro Dollars, EUR)

欧元是欧盟中 18 个国家的货币。欧元的 18 个会员国是爱尔兰、奥地利、比利时、德国、法国、芬兰、荷兰、卢森堡、葡萄牙、西班牙、希腊、意大利、斯洛文尼亚、塞浦路斯、马耳他、斯洛伐克、爱沙尼亚、拉脱维亚。1999 年 1 月 1 日,实行欧元的欧盟国家开始实行统一货币政策,2002 年 7 月欧元成为欧元区唯一合法货币。欧元由欧洲中央银行和各欧元区国家的中央银行组成的欧洲中央银行系统负责管理。总部坐落于德国法兰克福的欧洲中央银行有独立制定货币政策的权力,欧元区国家的中央银行参与欧元纸币和欧元硬币的印刷、铸造与发行,并负责欧元区支付系统的运作。

Euro Dollars(EUR) is the universe currency of the 18 countries in the European Union (EU) such as Ireland, Austria, Belgium, Germany, France, Finland, Netherlands, Luxembourg, Portugal, Spain, Greece, Italy, Slovenia, Cyprus, Malta, Slovakia, Estonia and Latvia. Those countries using EUR in EU implemented common monetary policy on January 1, 1999 and EUR became the only legal tender within the Euro Zone in July, 2002. EUR is under the control of the European Central Bank and European System of Central Banks (ESCB) made up of the central banks of its member countries. With Head Office located in Frankfurt, Germany, the European Central Bank has the independent power of enacting monetary policy while the Euro Zone member countries' central banks participate in the printing, casting and issuance of notes and coins as well as the operation of payment system in the Euro Zone.

1999 年 1 月 1 日,欧元在欧盟各成员国范围内正式发行,它是一种具有独立性和法定货币地位的超国家性质的货币,欧盟根据《马斯特里赫条约》规定,欧元于 2002 年 1 月 1 日起正式流通。自欧元创建以来,其纸币共有七种面额,分别是€5, €10,€20,€50,€100,€200 和€500。票面由窗户、大门和桥梁三个基本建筑要素构成,分别代表欧盟之间的开放、合作与沟通精神。第一套欧元纸币于 2002 年 1 月 1 日至 2013 年 5 月 1 日期间发行,随后在 2013 年 5 月 2 日起被第二套纸币所取代。与硬币不同的是，纸币的设计在整个欧元区都是一样的。为了使纸币更耐用，并使人们更容易地通过触摸来识别，印制纸币的纸张由纯棉纤维制造。欧元纸币的尺寸最小为 120 mm × 62 mm，最大为 160 mm × 82 mm；不同的纸币使用不同的主题色调以便区分。

As a super-state currency of independence and legal tender, EUR was officially issued within member countries of EU on January 1, 1999 and circulated officially from January 1, 2002 according to the regulations of *Treaty of Maastricht*. The notes have had seven denominations of Five Euro Dollars, Ten Dollars, Twenty Euro Dollars, Fifty Euro Dollars, One Hundred Euro Dollars, Two Hundred Euro Dollars and Five Hundred Euro Dollars since EUR was created. The face design of notes is composed of three basic building factors as window, gate and bridge, respectively representing opening, cooperation and communication among members of EU. The first set of EUR was released during the period from January 1, 2002 to May 1, 2013, and the second set of notes took the place subsequently from May 2, 2013. Different from coins, the design of the notes is the same in the whole Euro Zone. The paper used to print notes is made of pure cotton fiber in order to make the notes more durable and help people identify more easily by touching. The minimum size of Euro notes is 120 mm × 62 mm and the maximum size is 160 mm × 82 mm; different notes use different theme tones to tell from each other.

欧元是自罗马帝国以来欧洲货币改革最为重大的结果。欧元不仅仅使欧洲单一市场得以完善，欧元区国家间自由贸易更加方便，而且更是欧盟一体化进程的重要组成部分。

EUR has been the most important result of European monetary reform since Roman Empire. EUR not only makes the single market in Europe more perfect, facilitates the free trade between member countries in the Euro Zone, but also is the important part of the integration of the European Union.

2.7 货币欣赏（Appreciation of Currencies）

世界主要货币（Main Currencies）

Chinese Names	English Names	ISO Code	Symbol
美元	United States Dollars	USD	US $
欧元	Euro Dollars	EUR	€
英镑	British Pound	GBP	£
加拿大元	Canadian Dollars	CAD	Can $
日元	Japanese Yen	JPY	J ¥
澳大利亚元	Australian Dollars	AUD	A $
港币	Hong Kong Dollars	HKD	HK $
瑞士法郎	Swiss Franc	CHF	SF
新加坡元	Singapore Dollars	SGD	S $
新西兰元	New Zealand Dollars	NZD	NZ $
人民币元	Renminbi Yuans	CNY	RMB ¥

美元主要面值（Main Denominations of United States Dollars）

新版的 100 美元（The New 100 US Dollars）

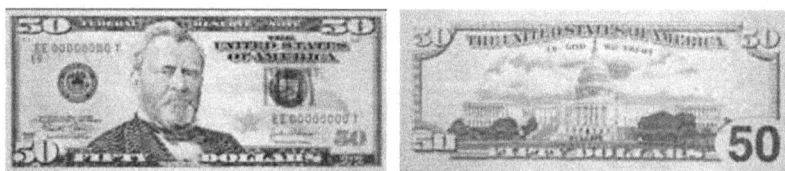

新版的 50 美元（The New 50 US Dollars）

新版的 20 美元（The New 20 US Dollars）

新版的 10 美元（The New 10 US Dollars）

英镑主要面值（Main Denominations of British Pounds）

50 英镑（Fifty Pounds）

20 英镑（Twenty Pounds）

10 英镑（Ten Pounds）

欧元主要面值(Main Denominations of Euro Dollars)

500 欧元(500 Euro Dollars)

200 欧元(200 Euro Dollars)

100 欧元(100 Euro Dollars)

50 欧元(50 Euro Dollars)

加拿大元主要面值(Main Denominations of Canadian Dollars)

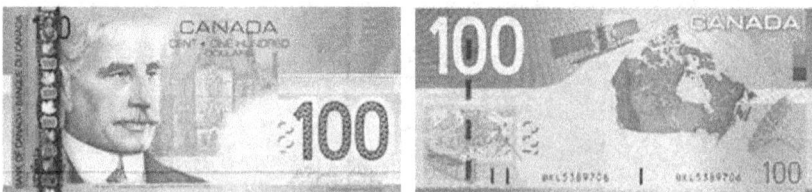

100 加拿大元（100 Canadian Dollars）

50 加拿大元（50 Canadian Dollars）

20 加拿大元（20 Canadian Dollars）

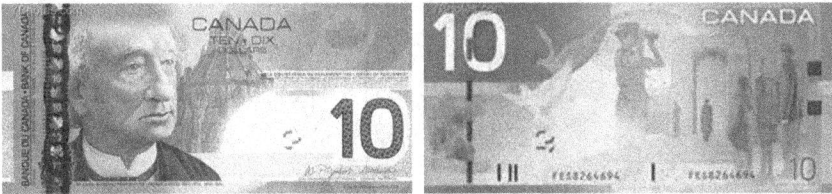

10 加拿大元（10 Canadian Dollars）

3 支付漫说
(Payment Stories)

3.0 导言（Introduction）

　　支付方式是指购物或消费需要付款形式的多种选择支付捷径。目前各个商家都有不同的支付方式，主要包括现金即时交易方式、货到付款支付方式、银行卡支付方式、第三方支付方式、转账支付等，本章主要介绍后三种支付方式。

　　Payment method refers to the way you choose to pay for your purchased goods or services. Different merchants have different ways to collect payment，which include cash transactions，cash on delivery，bank card payment，the third-party payment and wire transfer payment. This chapter mainly introduces the last three ones.

3.1 货到付款(Cash on Delivery)

概念(Definition)

　　货到付款在对外贸易中是指出口商先发出货物、进口商后付款的结算方式，此方式实际属于赊账交易或延期付款结算。电子商务（网上购物）中指的是由物流公司代收买家货款,货先送到客户手上,客户验货之后再把钱给送货员,也就是我们常说的"一手交钱一手交货",之后货款再转到卖家账户里去。货到付款可以开箱验货,先查看货物描述与购买的货物有无差别,检验货物真实性、质量运送损伤等之后,再根据情况签单。如果与事实不符,可以拒签,并表明理由。

Cash on delivery in foreign trade refers to the means of payments that the exporters send out the goods first before the importers pay. In fact, it is a kind of open account or deferred payment. But in e-commerce (on-line shopping), cash on delivery refers to businesses that the logistics companies first collect the payments from the buyer and then deliver the goods to the buyer, after the checking of the goods, the customers pay to the deliverymen as "cash on delivery", after that the money will be transferred to the seller's accounts. Cash on delivery allows customers to check and examine the goods, they may first check whether the goods are in compliance with the goods descriptions, examine the authenticity of the goods, the quality and the damages during the transportation and so on before they sign and pay. If there are any discrepancies, they can refuse to sign and state those reasons clearly.

业务流程(Business Procedures)

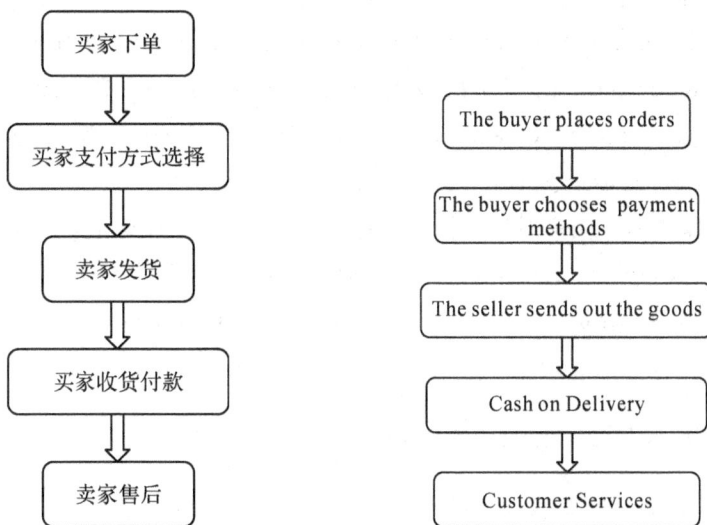

图 1　货到付款支付流程　　Figure 1　Procedures of Cash on Delivery

流程如下所示：

Procedures are as follows：

(1)买家下单。买家看中产品直接加入购物车或者直接快速订购。

(1) The buyer places orders. The buyer adds the goods into the shopping cart or places a quick order directly.

(2)买家支付方式选择。买家在支付方式选择上，选择货到付款。

(2) The buyer chooses payment methods. The buyer chooses cash on delivery as means of payment for the business.

(3)卖家发货。货到付款对卖家来说风险非常大，风险主要是来自一部分新手买家的恶意下单，然后拒收。这就给卖家增加了成本，成本高自然带动价格走高，买家就要多支付一笔钱。

(3) The seller sends out the goods. Cash on delivery will be a risk to the seller，which comes from the possibilities that the buyer will reject the commodities when they are delivered. This will increase costs for the seller，which will increase prices of these commodities. Thus，the buyer will have to pay extra money for commodities supporting cash on delivery.

(4)买家收货付款。物流公司把商品送到买家手上以后，买家进行验货，检查过商品没任何问题后再把货款交给物流人员，即完成了整个支付过程。

(4) The buyer pays after the arrival of the goods. After deliverymen deliver commodities，the buyer will check the qualities. If nothing is wrong with the goods，the buyer will sign for the goods and pay，which represents the completion of transactions.

(5)卖家售后。卖家对售后订单进行统一管理，做好退换货等售后服务。

(5) The seller offers customer services. The seller will make unified management for orders after being completed，and do a good job of after‐sales services as returns or exchanges.

支付优势(Payment Advantages)

货到付款的支付方式具有以下优势：

Cash on delivery has the following advantages：

(1)买家收到货物后付款，买家可以在验收货品满意后付款，提高了买家的满意度。

(1) The buyer can pay after the inspection of the goods, which increases the buyer's satisfaction significantly.

(2)货到付款增加了网购者对网购的信任度,便于发展诚信的网上购物。

(2) It can increase the credibility of online shoppers to develop the faithful online shopping.

(3)消费者和物流公司配送员见货后"钱货两清",避免了消费者和销售者之间的恶意纠纷。

(3) Payment will be cleared between consumers and deliverymen after the inspection of the goods in order to avoid the malicious disputes between the buyer and the seller.

(4)由于是物流配送人员收款,物流公司为了自己的利益,避免了野蛮装卸、野蛮运输,减少了货物在运输途中的损坏。

(4) Since the collection of payments is done by deliverymen, the logistics companies try to focus on avoiding the barbarous packing and transportation for the sake of themselves, which also decreases the damages of goods in transporting.

(5)增加了物流公司业务,拉动了就业,刺激了经济发展。

(5) It increases business volumes and employments for the logistics companies, which will stimulate the economy.

注意事项（Notice）

(1)验货注意事项

(1) Notices for Inspection of Goods

第一,当物流公司配送员派送货物时,买家应该先确认物流公司身份,是否与和卖家核实的一样,并查看运单号是否为网上显示的运单。若不同,千万不要收货,以免给自己、卖家及物流公司三方造成损失。

Firstly, after the deliverymen deliver the goods, the buyer should check the logistics companies' names and the tracking numbers to make sure all the information is correct, which will avoid costs resulting from wrong delivering.

第二,当确认货物为所订购宝贝后,先检查货物外包装及内物外观,在确定货物完好无损后,便可以签字并将代收款交予物流配送员。若发现货物与网站描述有差异,或者货物有破损应该立即拒绝签收,并立即联系卖家。

Secondly, the buyer should check the goods thoroughly to make sure they are in good quality. After the checking, the buyer can sign for the goods and pay for the delivery. If the goods are different from the description, the buyer should refuse to sign for them and contact the seller immediately.

第三,货到付款方式,无须再上网进行"确认收货"操作。

Thirdly, there is no need to confirm the receiving online if the cash on delivery method is adopted.

（2）回款周期事项

(2) Notices for the Payback Period

约为 T＋5 日。T 日（系指买家签收付款日）资金按以下方法进行清算。

The settlement time for the cash on delivery is about T＋5 days. T refers to the day the buyer signing for the goods and paying for them. The settlement for the payment has the following rules.

第一,如遇国家法定节假日,签收状态反馈时间及清算时间可能会顺延。

Firstly, the feedback of the goods delivering status will be delayed during national holidays.

第二,在物流公司将全额款项清算给卖家后的次日内,此时交易状态会变更为"交易成功"。

Secondly, after the clearing of the payment for the goods, the seller will receive the money and the status for the transaction will be "done."

（3）订单取消事项

(3) Notices for Order Canceling

买家选择货到付款购买后,如果想取消订单,建议买家及时联系卖家说明,可以通过阿里旺旺、邮件客服等给卖家留言,告知取消购买。若后续卖家强制发货,可以拒收。

If the buyer choose cash on delivery as the payment method and want to cancel the order, it is recommended to contact the seller through online chatting software like AliTM or email them to inform the canceling. If the seller insist on sending the goods to the buyer, it is fine for the buyer to the goods.

（4）配送其他事项

(4) Other Notices for the Delivery

第一,费用。有些"货到付款"支付方式,需要另外收取服务费,服务费根据货款金额的一定比例进行收取,有最低起步要求,上不封顶。

Firstly，it's about fee. Extra service fees may occur if the buyer chooses cash on delivery as the payment method，services fees will be a fraction to the payments，which will have a minimum threshold and no maximum threshold.

第二，时间。在买家选择货到付款方式购买宝贝后，卖家接到订单会在线下单通知物流取货，物流公司揽件成功录单后，交易状态会从"等待卖家发货"变更为"卖家已发货"，运送时间会根据物流公司的不同而有所不同，一般需要2—7天。

Secondly，it's time. After the buyer chooses cash on delivery as the payment method，the seller will contact the logistics company. After the logistics company accepts the goods，the status of the transaction will change from "pending" to "processing". It will take the logistics company 2 to 7 days to deliver the goods.

【操作小助手】淘宝商城"货到付款"方式操作流程

[Tips]The Operation Process of Cash on Delivery Payment Method in Taobao

①如果买家想使用货到付款服务，可以在搜索商品时，勾选货到付款选项，筛选结果全部是支持货到付款的商品；此流程适用于淘宝网上的商品。

① If the buyer wants to use cash on delivery as the payment method，it is recommended to check the "Cash on Delivery" option box，the search results will be commodities that support this delivery method；this process is applied to all commodities in Taobao.

图2 "货到付款"商家查询

Figure 2　Search Traders Have the Option of Cash on Delivery

②支持货到付款的商品,页面会有明显的提醒。

②Commodities supporting the cash on delivery method have the option mark showing below.

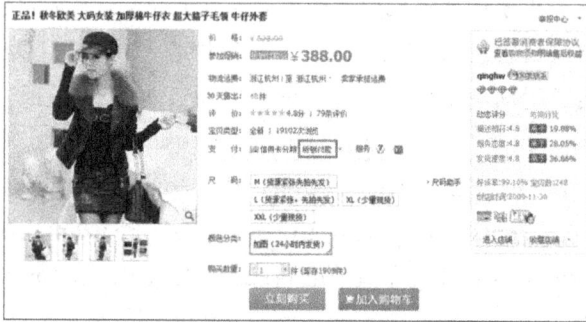

图3 "货到付款"支付方式提醒

Figure 3 Reminder of Cash on Delivery Payment Method

③购买单件商品点击"立刻购买",选择"运送方式"为货到付款。买家可以按服务费进行相应的选择。

③After choosing "Cash on Delivery" as the "Delivery Method", the buyer can make decisions based on service fees.

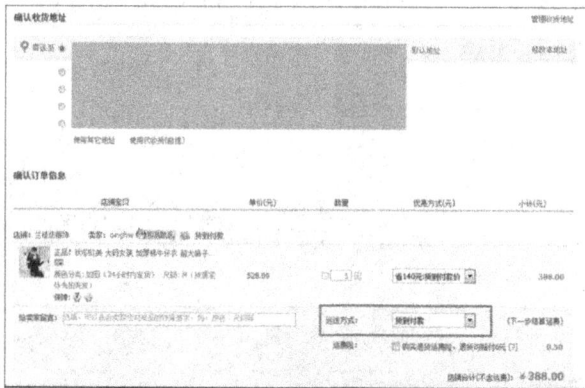

图4 "货到付款"运送方式选择

Figure 4 Choosing Cash on Delivery as the Option

④点击"下一步",付款方式选择"现金支付"——"提交订单",即完成线上下单流程。

④You can click the button Next, choose Cash Payment as the payment method and then submit the order. It means the ordering on line process has been completed.

图5 "货到付款"付款方式选择

Figure 5   Choosing the Option of Cash on Delivery Payment Method

⑤下单后,买家即可在家等待物流公司送货上门。为了保证货物顺利送达,请买家务必确保联系电话畅通。

⑤In order to have the goods delivered,it is better for the buyer to make sure they can be contacted by phone.

【操作小助手】京东商城"货到付款"方式操作流程

[Tips]The Operation Process of Cash on Delivery in JD.COM

①登录买家的京东账户,进入京东商城的首页。

①The buyer can enter the front page of JD.com and log into his or her JD account.

图6 京东商城首页

Figure 6   The Front Page of JD.COM

②将京东商城的首页拉到最下面,买家就能看到"支付方式"。点击支付方式中的"货到付款"选项。

②At the bottom of JD.COM, the buyer will find Payment Methods where they can choose the option of Cash on Delivery.

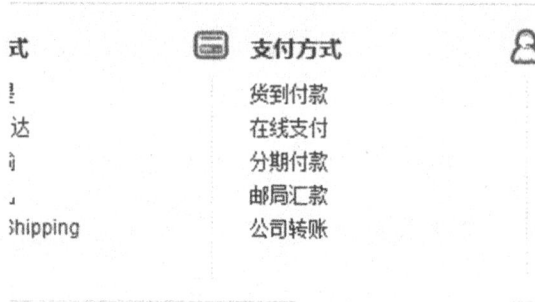

图7 京东商城"支付方式"选择

Figure 7 Choosing Payment Methos at JD. COM

④点击"货到付款"之后,买家就可以开始购物了。选择自己喜欢的商品加入购物车。

④If the buyer's location supports the Cash on Delivery method，the buyer can start shopping being aware of this. The buyer can add what he or she likes into the shopping cart.

图8 京东商城商品选购

Figure 9 Shopping Commodities at JD. COM

⑤然后买家进入自己的购物车中,选中自己需要购买的商品,点击"结算"。

⑤The buyer can select commodities he or she wants to buy at the shopping cart and click the Checking Out button.

图9 京东商城商品结算

Figure 9 Checking Out at JD. COM

⑥进入结算页面之后，填写完自己的寄送地址之后。选择"提交订单"就好了。收到货后，买家把货款交给物流配送员就完成了交易过程。

⑥The buyer can enter the shipping address at the checking out page and click the Submitting Order button. After the buyer receives commodities，they can do payments with deliverymen to complete the shopping process.

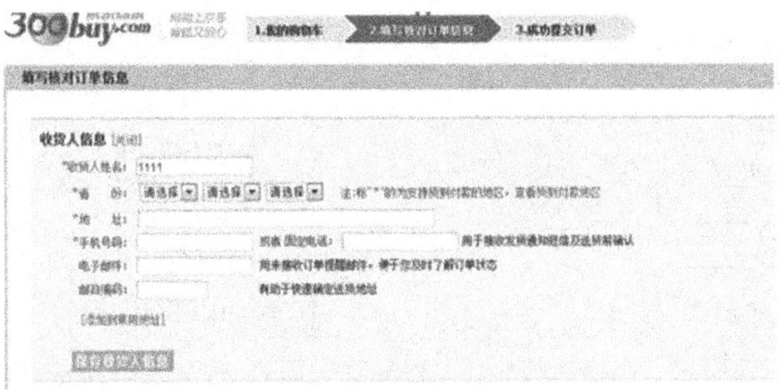

图 10　京东商城商品订单提交

Figure 10　Submitting Order at JD. COM

3.2 银行卡支付（**Bank Card Payment**）

概念（Definition）

银行卡支付（此处的银行卡支付主要是指银行卡线下支付）是买家在支付结算时，借助银行卡通过 POS 刷卡、RFID 机拍卡、手工压单、预授权等方式，向卖家账户支付的一种结算方式。银行卡支付方式在付款成功后，所支付的款项将立刻进入商家提供的账户。银行卡支付方式比较灵活，使用范围比较广，在欧美发达国家比较流行。

The bank card payment（mainly refers to off-line payment）refers to the buyer swiping cards through POS terminal machine，RFID machine，manual operation or preauthorization to do the payment. Money will be settled to the the seller's account after the payment has been processed. The bank card payment method is flexible and popular，especially in western countries.

业务流程（Service Processes）

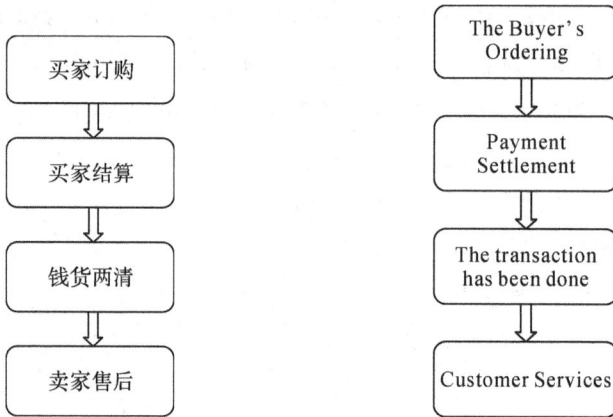

图 11　银行卡线下支付流程　　Figure 11　Process of the Off-line Bank Card Payment

（1）买家订购。买家进行商品购物或其他消费。

(1) The buyer's ordering. The buyer purchases commodities and services.

（2）买家结算。买家在支付方式选择上，选择银行卡支付方式，然后通过 POS 刷卡、RFID 机拍卡、手工压单、预授权等方式，向卖家账户进行支付的结算。

(2) Payment settlement. The buyer swipes cards through POS terminal machine，RFID machine，manual operation or preauthorization to do the payment.

（3）钱货两清。银行卡线下交易中，买家通过刷卡方式结算，直接完成交易过程，钱货两清。

(3) The transaction has been done. The buyer swipes cards to do the settlement. The transaction will be done after the swiping.

（4）卖家售后。卖家提供商品售后服务或提供其他相关服务。

(4) Customer services. The seller provides customer services and other relevant services.

支付优势（Payment Advantages）

（1）银行卡是当今发展最快的金融业务之一，它是一种可在一定范围内替代传统现金流通的电子货币。

(1) The service of bank cards service is one of the most pronounced

financial services. Electronic money can be a substitute for cash。

（2）银行卡是集金融业务与电脑技术于一体的高科技产物。

（2）Bank cards are high-tech products relying on computer technics and financial services.

（3）银行卡能减少现金货币的使用。

（3）Bank cards can decrease the usage of currency.

（4）银行卡能提供结算服务,方便购物消费,增强安全感。

（4）Bank cards can provide settlement services to make shopping much more convenient.

（5）银行卡能简化收款手续,节约社会劳动力。

（5）Bank cards can simplify the process of payment and save human resource costs.

（6）银行卡能促进商品销售,刺激消费。

（6）Bank cards can prosper commodity market and stimulate consumption.

（7）信用卡同时具有支付和信贷两种功能。持卡人可用其购买商品或享受服务,还可通过使用信用卡从发卡机构获得一定的贷款。

（7）Credit cards have functions of payments and financial credits. Cardholders can use credit cards to purchase products and obtain loans.

【小贴士】信用卡交易弊端

[Tips]Disadvantages of Credit Cards

信用卡的发明像一把双刃剑,可以解决经济上的暂时危机,但银行发行信用卡的目的是赚钱,一旦超过无息还款的时间,就会收取高额的利息,一般是每天万分之五的利息。

Credit cards can provide lots of convenience for the society, however, the bank will charge high fees if the cardholder have not paid back before the due day, which will be 0.5‰ per day.

①盲目消费:刷卡不像付现金那样一张一张把钞票花出去,容易导致盲目消费。

①Aimless consumption：Consumers intend to consume more with cards since they do not see the cash taking out from their own purses.

②过度消费:笔记本分期,数码相机分期,智能手机分期,在提前享用自己心仪物品的同时,还要考虑是否有能力偿还。

②Excess consumption：Installment payments are available for purchasing laptops, cameras and smartphones. It is recommended to take your consumption abilities into consideration before the purchasing.

③利息高：如果你不会打理信用卡，导致最后还款日到了也不能如期还款，银行会向你收取高额利息。

③The higher interest rate：Banks will charge higher interest rates if you pay back your credit card after the due date.

④需交年费：信用卡基本上都有年费，但基本上都有免年费的政策，比如中国建设银行一年只要刷三次就可以免年费。

④Annual fees：Annual fees are applied to most credit cards. Each bank has its annual fee waiving policy；for example，the China Construction Bank can waive your annual fee if you use your credit card at least three times per year.

⑤盗刷：信用卡基本上默认是免密码刷卡消费的，这就很容易在丢失或被盗时被别人盗刷，造成不必要的麻烦或损失；建议信用卡申请凭密。

⑤Credit card steeling：Unnecessary trouble and losses will occur if credit cards are lost since newly issued credit cards can be used without entering passcodes. It is recommended to set a passcode each credit card.

⑥影响个人信用记录：长期恶意欠款，自然会影响个人信用记录，甚至被银行打入黑名单，以后要向银行贷款，就有可能被银行拒绝。

⑥Bad influence toward credit records：Someone will have a bad credit record or be listed in the blacklist by the bank if he fails to pay back the credit card for a long time. Then，it will be very difficult for the person to get mortgages.

⑦注销麻烦：中国中央电视台曾报道过，曾有持卡人注销信用卡后仍收到银行账单。这篇报道揭露了现今信用卡的弊端。

⑦Troubles canceling cards：CCTV used to report that one cardholder still received credit card bills after he canceled the credit card，which revealed problems of credit cards regulations.

交易方式 (Trading Methods)

（1）POS 机刷卡（POS Terminal Machine）

在 POS 机上刷卡是最常见的银行卡使用方式，是一种联网刷卡的方式。刷卡时，操作员应首先查看银行卡的有效期和持卡人姓名等信息。然后，根据发卡行和需要支付的货币种类选择相应的 POS 机，将磁条式银行卡的磁条在 POS 机上划过，或者将芯片式银行卡插入卡槽，联通银行等支付网关，输入相应的金额。远程支付网关接受信息后，POS 机会打出刷卡支付的收据，持卡人检查支付收据上的信息无误后应在此收据上签字。操作员核对收据上的签名和银行卡背后的签名后，将银行卡及刷卡支付收据的客户联还给持卡人，至此，POS 机上的刷卡程序完成。具体流程如图 12 所示。

Bank card consumption using POS terminal machines has become more and more popular. The cashier should check the validity of the card and the name of the cardholder first. Then the cashier can choose the right type of POS terminal machine based on the type of the card and the currency. The POS terminal machine will connect to the bank gateway after the card swiping. The cashier can enter the money amount of the commodities. After the remote payment gateway receives the information about the payment, receipts will be printed out. The cardholder can sign on his or her signature after checking the receipt. The cashier should check the signature before giving the cardholder the receipt. The process of using POS machine is shown as Figure 12.

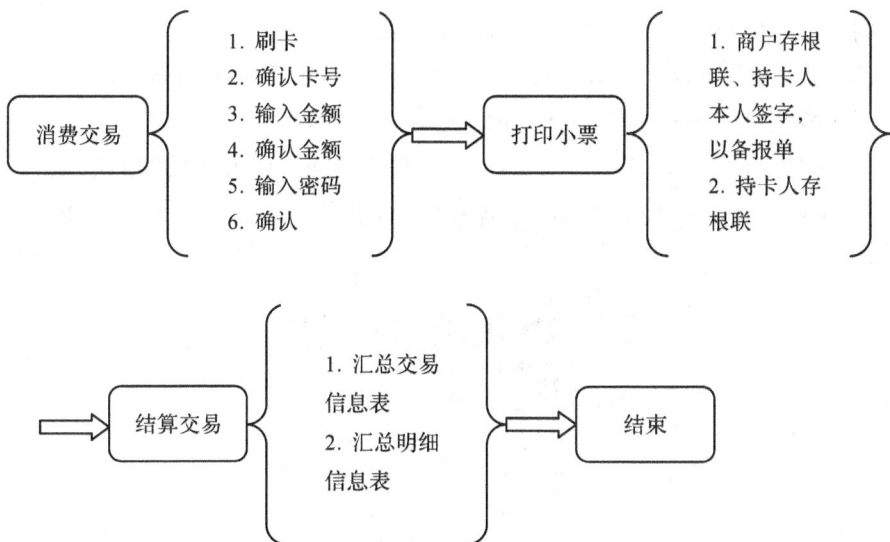

图 12　银行卡 POS 支付流程

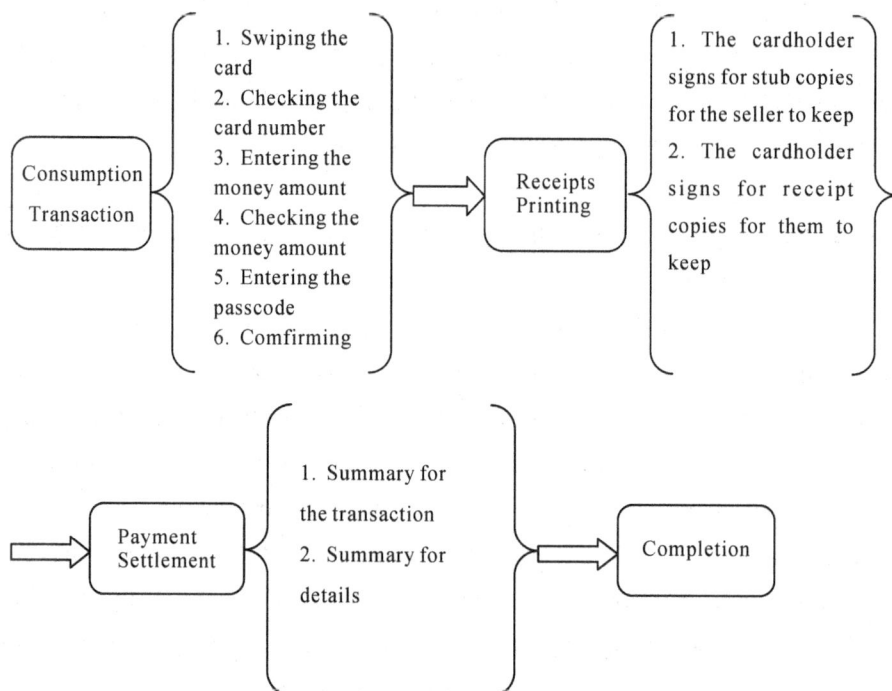

```
┌──────────────┐     ┌─ 1. Swiping the      ┌──────────────┐     ┌─ 1. The cardholder
│ Consumption  │     │    card              │              │     │    signs for stub copies
│ Transaction  │─────┤ 2. Checking the      │  Receipts    │─────┤    for the seller to keep
└──────────────┘     │    card number       │  Printing    │     │ 2. The cardholder
                     │ 3. Entering the      └──────────────┘     │    signs for receipt
                     │    money amount                           │    copies for them to
                     │ 4. Checking the                           └─   keep
                     │    money amount
                     │ 5. Entering the
                     │    passcode
                     └─ 6. Comfirming
```

```
        ┌──────────────┐     ┌─ 1. Summary for      ┌──────────────┐
───────▶│  Payment     │     │    the transaction   │              │
        │  Settlement  │─────┤ 2. Summary for       │  Completion  │
        └──────────────┘     └─   details           └──────────────┘
```

Figure 12 Payment Process Using POS Machine

【操作小助手】银行卡 POS 机刷卡操作流程

[Tips] The Process of Swiping Cards Using POS Terminal Machine

①消费交易（Consumption Transaction）

第一,刷卡消费。将银行卡磁条向下（一般朝内侧）,刷卡,如图 13 所示。

Firstly, you should put the magnetic strip down and swipe as shown in Figure 13.

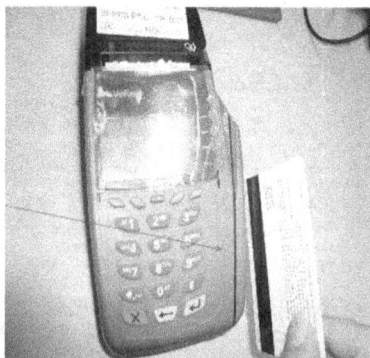

图 13 银行卡刷卡消费

Figure 13 Swiping Cards to Consume

第二，确认卡号。POS 机屏幕显示卡号，收款人核对显示卡号是否正确，按确认键，如图 14 所示。

Secondly，the screen of the POS terminal machine will show the card number，the payer should check the card number and press the correct button if the number is right as shown in Figure 14.

图 14 确认卡号

Figure 14 Checking Card Number

第三，输入金额。输入收款金额，核对是否正确，按确认键，如图 15 所示。

Thirdly，the payer should enter the money amount after inputting the amount and pressing the correct button if the amount is right as Figure 15 shows.

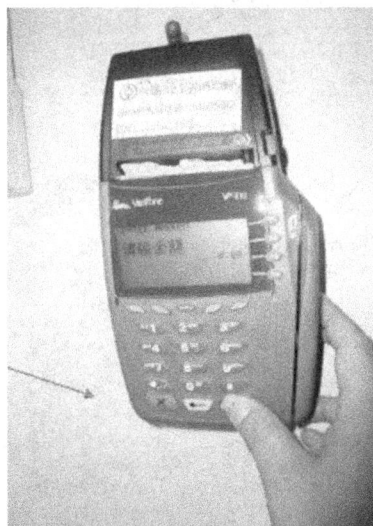

图 15 输入金额

Figure 15 Inputting Money Amount

第四，输入密码。输入持卡人密码，按确认键，如图 16 所示。

Fourthly, the cardholder should type the password and press the correct button as Figure 16 shows.

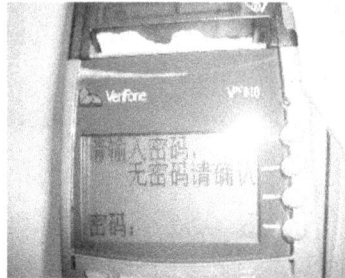

图 16　输入密码

Figure16　Inputting Password

②打印小票（Receipts Printing）

两联银行小票。交易成功，POS 机打印两联签购单，请持卡人签名。持卡人须核对卡号、金额是否正确。"持卡人存根联"交客户；"商户存根联"留存，以备报单，如图 17 所示。

The POS terminal machine will print one receipt copy and one stub copy for the cardholder to sign. Cardholders should check the card number and money amount before signing. The consumer will keep the receipt copy and the seller will keep the stub copy. The process is shown in Figure 17.

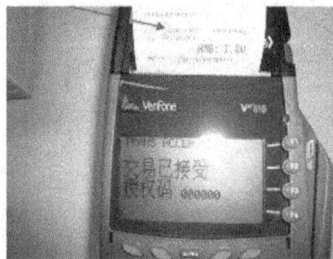

图 17　打印小票

Figure 17　Printing Receipts

③结算交易（Payment Settlement）

选"结算交易"，确认；POS机自动打印汇总交易结算信息；按提示，选择是否打印汇总明细，确认；按提示，是否删除流水信息（删除后，开始重新汇总，不删除自动累计，三日内自动删除），如图18所示。

The POS terminal machine will do the summary about all the transactions after choosing and confirming Payment Settlement. Following the instructions, the cashier can choose whether to print out these transaction statements or not, as well as whether to delete these statements or not（After the deleting, there will be a new summary and an automatic deleting process in three days）. It's shown in Figure 18.

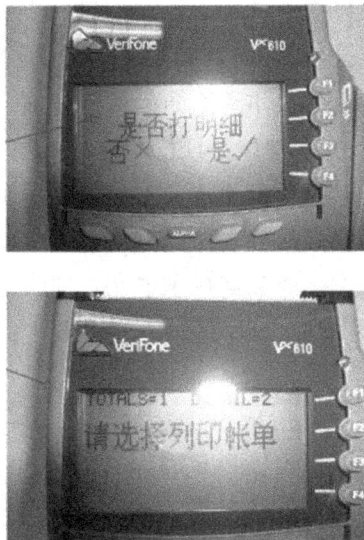

图 18　结算交易
Figure 18　Payment Settlement

（2）RFID 机拍卡（RFID Machine）

在 RFID 机上以"拍卡"感应是一种新类型的信用卡使用方式。拍卡时，操作员应首先查看信用卡的有效期和持卡人姓氏等信息。然后，根据发卡行和需要支付的货币种类选择相应的拍卡机，将信用卡平放于感应器上方不多于 10cm 的地方。RFID 机感应到信用卡后会发出讯号声响，然后继续运作程序，远程支付网关接受信息后，打印机会打出拍卡支付的收据。但持卡人无须签字，比以往的方式更快捷、更方便。

There are inductors in RFID machines to sense credit cards. Before using the RFID machine to collect payments for commodities, the cashier should check the validity of the card and the name of the cardholder. Then the cashier will choose the right type of RFID machine based on the type of the card and the currency. After putting cards on top of the RFID machines no more than 10cm and sensing these cards, the RFID machine will give signal. After the remote payment gateway receives all the information about the payment, receipts will be printed out. However, the cardholder does not need to sign for receipts, which makes the process more convenient and faster.

（3）手工压单（Manual Operation）

手工压单通常在没有 POS 机或不能联网的情况下使用。压单操作必须有压敏复写式的"直接签购单"（至少是两联）和电话。压单前的检查工作与 POS 机相同。然后，操作员用压单设备将信用卡上凸起的卡号、姓名等印到签购单上，并书写金额、日期等资讯，然后拨打收单银行授权专线电话，报出卡片资讯申请授权，并将获得的授权码书写在签购单上，然后持卡人确认无误后签字。操作员核对签名后，将信用卡和签购单的一联交给持卡人，至此，手工压单程序完成。在某些通信不畅或信用风纪良好的地区，会遇到商户压卡客户签字后便交付商品完成交易的情况，授权会在日后完成，可能导致损失（如若客户使用无效卡支付，不立即申请授权码便无法马上发现）。

Manual operation is used when POS terminal machines are not available or cannot be connected to the network. Receipt copies/stub copies and telephone numbers will be needed for the manual operation. The checking process is similar to that using POS terminal machine. The cashier will make a print of the card number and the name by pressing the card against the copy paper. After writing the money amount and the date and contact the bank by dialing authorized number, the cashier will get authorization from the bank by giving the card information. The cashier will get a serial number. By writing the serial number on the copy paper and making sure the cardholder's signature is correct, cashier can give the receipt copy to the cardholder and complete the manual operation process. At areas that have bad signals or great credit reputations, the seller may not contact the bank to get authorization, which will confront a loss (If the card is invalid, the payment will not be settled to the seller's account）.

【知识链接】手工压单方式

[Links] Ways To Do the Manual Operation

免授权的压印方式

Ways To Do the Authorization-free Manual Operation

这种压印方式是指在商户协议规定的授权底限以内，免授权进行的压卡交易。具体操作流程如下：

Under certain situations，it is fine to process the payment without the bank's authorization. The process is shown as below：

①判断受理交易的金额是否在授权底限内；

① the cashier should check whether the money amount is valid for authorization-free manual operation；

②通过多种渠道（电话银行、POS机、书面黑名单、授权电话）验证该卡是否列入黑名单；

②the cashier should check whether the card is on the blacklist through different channels（telephone banks，the POS terminal machine，the written blacklist，the authorized telephone checking）；

③压印；

③the cashier can make prints of the card；

④将商户名称代号和交易金额填于签购单的相应栏；

④ the cashier can put the merchant's name and money amount into the copy paper；

⑤签字；

⑤the cardholder can sign these copies；

⑥核对签名无误后，将卡片和持卡人存根联交持卡人，留下其他几联单据，最后将相关材料在收单机构规定的时限内送收单机构清算。

⑥after making sure the signature is correct，the cashier will give the card and the receipt copy to the cardholder and keep other copies. Then，the cashier will give relevant materials to the bank to do the payment settlement.

逐笔获取授权的压印方式

Ways To Get Authorization for Every Transaction

这种压印方式是指无论交易金额大小，收银员均需按照受理协议所规定的授权途径和联系方式向发卡机构或收单机构逐笔索取授权的压印交易。在 POS 出现故障无法使用或通信线路故障时,可采取这种方式,具体操作流程如下:

Under this situation, the cashier should get authorization from the bank issuing the card according to the authorization ways and contact methods stipulated by acceptance agreement no matter how small the money amount is. It is recommended to use this method when the POS machine has some problems or the signal is bad. The process is shown as below:

①索取人工授权;

①ask for authorization;

②压印;

②mak mould printing;

③将商户名称代号、授权号码和交易金额填于签购单的相应栏内;

③write merchant's name, authorized serial number and money amount at the copy paper;

④持卡人签字;

④sign;

⑤核对无误后,将卡片和持卡人存根联交持卡人,留下其他几联单据,最后将相关材料在收单机构规定的时限内送收单机构清算。

⑤after making sure the signature is correct, the cashier will give the card and receipt copy to the cardholder and keep the other copies, and give relevant materials to the bank to do the payment settlement.

(4)预授权(Preauthorization)

预授权一般用于支付押金,即冻结一部分信用卡的可用额度,当作押金。预授权和手工压单的过程类似,但是电话内容是要求预授权相应的金额,不是要求支付,也不需要压单。一般结账的时候由商家取消预授权。如果商家忘记取消,可以打电话给商家要求取消,自己打电话给授权机构无法取消。或者,等待银行自动取消预授权(一般情况为7—30天)。

The preauthorization is used by freezing parts of credit card's credit limit as deposits. The process of the preauthorization is similar to that of the manual operation. The difference is that the preauthorization will ask authorization for certain amount of money; it is not about the payment and there is no need to do the mould printing. Merchants will cancel the preauthorization when customers decide to check out. If merchants forget to cancel the preauthorization, customers can inform merchants to do it because customers cannot cancel it by calling the bank. Or, they can wait for the bank to cancel it automatically (usually it will take 7 to 30 days).

【案例链接】

［Case Study］

某日李女士为客户定房一间,使用本人牡丹卡为其担保,预定时银行方进行了预授权 1000 元的处理,李女士要求客户离店结清账务后通知并取消此笔授权。在李女士的客户结账离店时,为提高效率,中国工商银行工作人员向客户商量取消李女士的信用卡授权采用交易 0.01 的方式（预授权完成结算）快捷,李女士的客户欣然同意,并答应把单子交给李女士告知此事。事后李女士对此事很不满意,理由:第一,未经本人同意;第二,这样操作很不严谨,使她很担心,这并不是 0.01 的问题,而是性质问题。

Ms. Li used her peony credit card to pay for her clients when she ordered hotels for them. When she did the reservation, the bank preauthorized RMB 1000. Ms. Li told her clients to cancel the preauthorization and inform her after checking out. However, Ms. Li's customers agreed to use the method of authorization with 0.01 interest rates to cancel the preauthorization and promised to inform Ms. Li later. Ms. Li was not satisfied with the results, because she was not informed before the method was used and the operation is not precise as well, which is not just a money issue.

分析:虽然银行这样操作是为了更好地提高服务效率,但在此过程中却疏忽了一个重要问题——未经本人同意。李女士的意见很有道理,这不仅仅是一分钱的问题,还是关系到客户个人权利的问题,必须引起重视 。

Case Review:The bank used the method to cancel the preauthorization in order to improve the efficiency, but they made a big mistake—failing to inform Ms. Li. So, it is not only an issue about money, but also an issue of the personal rights of clients.

【小贴士】信用卡分期付款

［Tips］Installment Payments for Credit Cards

信用卡分期付款就是指持卡人使用信用卡进行大额消费时,由发卡银行向商户一次性支付持卡人所购商品（或服务）的消费资金,并根据持卡人申请,将消费资金分期通过持卡人信用卡账户扣收,持卡人按照每月入账金额进行偿还的业务。

The installment payment for the credit card refers to the method that the cardholder can use the credit card to buy expensive goods and use the installment payment to pay back the credit card.

绝大多数都有信用卡分期付款业务分期付款一般根据场合的不同分为商场(POS)分期、邮购分期与账单分期。信用卡还款方式见表 1 所示。

Most banks have the installment payment business. The installment payment business can be divided into the POS installment payment，the mailing installment payment and financing installment. The payments for credit cards are shown as following：

表 1 信用卡还款方式一览表

还款方式	还款说明
发卡行内还款	该方式包括：发卡行柜台、自助柜员机、网上银行、自动转账、电话银行还款等方式。还款后,信用卡额度即时恢复。
微银 POS 手机还款	微银通 POS 手机是一种移动金融系统个人支付终端,既可以用来直接刷卡还款,也可以进行转账等业务。即时到账。
转账/汇款还款	主要分为：同城跨行、异地跨行等两种方式。无论是何种方式进行转账或者汇款,汇出行将收取一定的费用,同时款项在到账的时间和还款便捷程度上都不如同行内还款、网络还款、便利店还款等方式。
网络还款	国内比较常见的网络平台有银联在线、快钱、盛付通、支付宝、财付通等。选择不同的平台和银行,收费标准和款项具体到账时间均有所不同。
便利店还款	该种方式主要是通过安装在便利店中的"拉卡拉"智能支付终端完成还款,一般到账时间需 2—3 个工作日,同时利用这种方式还款免收取手续费。
柜面通还款	柜面通指各联网金融机构发行的银行卡,通过在银联交换中心主机系统注册的他行银行网点柜面,进行人民币活期存取款交易。
信付通还款	"信付通"智能刷卡电话是中国银联自主研发,通过银行卡检测中心认证,并由中国银联跨行信息交换网络提供金融服务支持的创新电子产品。
其他方式	除了上面提到的几种方式外,发卡行为了便于持卡人还款,还开通了各自特色的还款方式。

Table 1　Payment for Credit Cards

Payment Methods	Payment Instructions
Repayment in the Issuing Bank	This method includes repayments through counters at the issuing bank，ATM，online bank，automatic transferring and the telephone bank. After the repayment，the credit card will have a zero balance.
Wing Mobile Payment	The wing mobile repayment is a method using the financial individual mobile terminal，which can be used as a POS machine to swipe cards or do wire transfer as well. The settlement will be done immediately.
Repayment Through Wire Transfer	It includes regional cross-bank wire transfer and remote cross-bank wire transfer service. Both methods will occur fees. It is not as convenient and as quick as inner bank repayment，online repayment and convenient store repayment.
Online Repayment	There are many payment platforms as Union Pay，Alipay，Tenpay and so on. Choosing different platforms and banks will occur different amount of fees.
Convenient Store Repayment	This method will allow you to do the repayment through the Lakala terminal installed at the convenient store，which usually will take 2—3 business days to do the settlement and is fee-free.
Counter Pass Service Repayment	The counter pass service repayment refers to doing the repayment at bank branches registered at Union Pay Transfer Center System.
Credit Repayment Through Anypay	The Union Pay develops the credit repayment through. The Union Pay Information Transfer Network will provide financial service to complete the repayment.
Other Methods	There are other different repayment methods available.

3.3 第三方支付 (Third-Party Payment)

概念(Definition)

第三方支付是买家在支付结算时，借助银行卡通过第三方支付平台，完成交易的一种结算方式。在通过第三方支付平台的交易中，买方选购商品后，使用第三方平台提供的账户进行货款支付，由第三方通知卖家货款到达、进行发货；买方检验物品后，就可以通知付款给卖家，第三方再将款项转至卖家账户。

The third-party payment refers to buyers using the third-party payment platforms to do the payment settlements. Buyers select commodities and use the payment platforms. The third-party payment platforms will inform sellers to send out commodities. After buyers will check commodities and authorize payments to sellers, payments will be transfewed to sellers' accounts.

支付流程(Payment Procedures)

在第三方支付交易流程中,支付模式使商家看不到客户的信用卡信息,同时又避免了信用卡信息在网络上多次公开传输而导致信用卡信息被窃。

Using the third-party payment make it impossible for the merchant to have the access to customers' credit card information. It avoids credit card information leakage.

以 B2C 交易为例,见图 19 所示。

Let us use B2C as an example as Figure 19 shows.

(1)客户(买方)在电子商务网站上选购商品,最后决定购买,买卖双方在网上达成交易意向。

(1) Customers (buyers) will select commodities online and place the order;

(2)客户选择利用第三方作为交易中介,客户用信用卡将货款划到第三方账户;

(2) customers will select the third-party payment as the medium of transaction and deposit the transaction amount to the third-party payment platform account;

(3)第三方支付平台将客户已经付款的消息通知商家,并要求商家在规定时间内发货;

(3) the third-party payment platform will inform the seller of the depositing of payment and the seller will send out commodities within a certain time lock;

(4)商家收到通知后按照订单发货;

(4) sellers send out commodities;

(5)客户收到货物并验证后通知第三方;

(5) commodities will be delivered and buyers will check commodities. If everything is fine, buyers will inform the third-party payment;

(6)第三方将其账户上的货款划入商家账户中,交易完成。

(6) the third-party payment will settle the transaction payment to sellers' accounts.

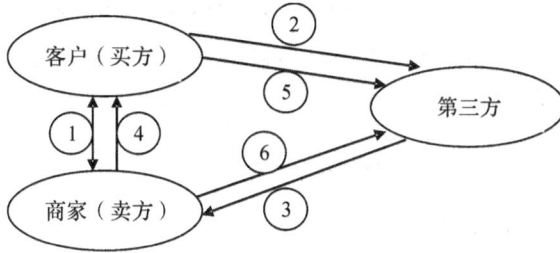

图 19 第三方支付流程

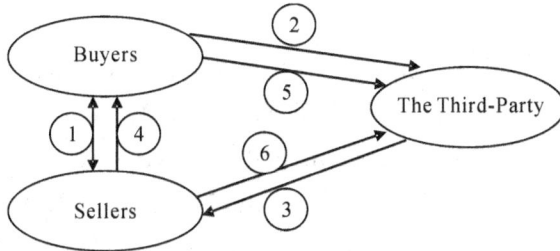

Figure 19 The Third-Party Payment Procedure

支付特点（Payment Characteristics）

（1）第三方支付平台提供一系列的应用接口程序，将多种银行卡支付方式整合到一个界面上，负责交易结算中与银行的对接，使网上购物更加快捷、便利。

(1) The third-party payment platform provides a series of programs to put all the bank cards payment to a page to connect with all banks to do the settlement，which makes the online shopping more convenient and quicker.

（2）较之 SSL、SET 等支付协议，利用第三方支付平台进行支付操作更加简单而且易于接受。借助第三方支付平台，商家和客户之间的交涉由第三方来完成，使网上交易变得更加简单。

(2) Compared to SSL and SET and other payment contracts，the third-party payment is easier，because buyers and sellers only deal with the third-party payment platform.

（3）第三方支付平台本身依附于大型的门户网站，且以与其合作的银行的信用作为信用依托，因此第三方支付平台能够较好地突破网上交易中的信用问题，有利于推动电子商务的快速发展。

(3) The third-party payment platform usually relies on the portal website and is secured by the reputation of its cooperation banks. This will help to boost the electronic commerce.

支付优势(Payment Advantages)

第三方支付模式有效地保障了交易各方的利益,为整个交易的顺利进行提供了支持。

The third-party payment method guarantees all parties' interests, which makes the transaction more reliable.

(1)支付安全。信用卡信息或账户信息仅需要告知支付中介,而无须告诉每一个收款人,这大大减少了信用卡信息和账户信息失密的风险。

(1) Only the third-party payment platform will have access to customers' credit card information, which decreases the information leakage risk.

(2)支付成本较低。支付中介集中了大量的电子小额交易,形成规模效应,因而支付成本较低。

(2) The transaction cost is lower. Payment intermediaries concentrate lots of small electronic transactions, forming a scale effect, so the cost of payment is lower.

(3)使用方便。对支付者而言,他所面对的是友好的界面,不必考虑背后复杂的技术操作过程。

(3) It is easy to use. For the payer, he faces a friendly interface and does not have to take into account the complex technological process behind it.

(4)支付担保业务可以在很大程度上保障付款人的利益。

(4)The payment guarantee services secure the payment.

支付品牌(Platform Brands)

中国国内的第三方支付产品主要有支付宝、拉卡拉、财付通、宝付等。

Alipay, Lakala, Tenpay and Baofoo are the famous third-party payment platforms in China.

支付宝(Alipay)

支付宝(中国)网络技术有限公司是国内领先的独立第三方支付平台,由阿里巴巴集团在 2004 年 12 月创立,是阿里巴巴集团的关联公司。支付宝致力于为中国电子商务提供"简单、安全、快速"的在线支付解决方案。

Alipay is the most famous third-party payment platform in China，which is created by Alibaba in December，2004 and a related company to Alibaba. The company culture is to provide "simple，convenient，quick" online payment services.

拉卡拉支付（Lakala）

拉卡拉集团是首批获得央行颁发《支付业务许可证》的第三方支付公司，是中国最大的便民金融服务公司，联想控股成员企业。致力于为个人和企业提供日常生活所必须的金融服务及生活、网购、信贷等增值服务。2013年8月完成集团化结构调整，下设拉卡拉支付公司、拉卡拉移动公司、拉卡拉商服、拉卡拉销售和拉卡拉电商公司。

The Lakala Group is the first third-party payment platform getting third-party payment license，which is hold by Lenovo. Lakala insists on providing financial services for the public，including online shopping services and loans services. The Lakala Group has been divided into Lakala Payment Company，Lakala mobile company and Lakala electronic commerce company in August，2013.

财付通（Tenpay）

财付通是腾讯公司于2005年9月正式推出的专业在线支付平台，致力于为互联网用户和企业提供安全、便捷、专业的在线支付服务。

Tenpay is the third-party payment platform developed by Tencent in September，2005，which provides safe，quick and sophisticated online payment services.

宝付（Baofoo）

宝付推出的"我的支付导航"主要分个人支付导航与商户支付导航两大板块。宝付提供从网上交水电煤等基本生活需要，到旅行买机票、买火车票、定酒店，再到网上购物、通讯充值等各种类型"日常便民服务"，"我的支付导航"不仅为广大个人用户提供了便利的生活支付服务，也给企业商户提供行业解决方案、一站式的解决方案及增值服务等产品服务。

Baofoo has the payment navigation service，which includes the individual payment navigation and the merchant payment navigation. This service covers services connected to routine life as paying electricity and water bills to ticket booking and online shopping. It provides one-stop services for everybody as well.

【操作小助手】淘宝(支付宝)银行卡添加与修改操作流程

[Tips]Debit or Credit Card Adding and Revising Process at Taobao. com (Alipay)

由于淘宝与支付宝绑定,淘宝上是不能直接添加银行卡的,只能在支付宝添加,但是可从淘宝进入支付宝相关页面添加银行卡,也可直接进入支付宝添加。此经验选择第一种方式,即从淘宝进入添加,步骤如下。

Since Taobao can be bound with Alipay but cannot with bank cards，the only way to bind taobao with bank cards is through Alipay. The process is shown as below.

①打开淘宝网站:www. taobao. com,登录,如图 20 所示。

① Open website：www. taobao. com and log in as Figure 20 shows.

图 20　淘宝登录界面

Figure 20　The Logging Page of Taobao. com

②登录后,点击导航栏"我的淘宝",此时进入如图 21 所示页面。

②After logging in，you can click My Taobao at the navigation bar and enter the page as Figure 21 shows.

图 21 "我的淘宝"界面

Figure 21   The Page of My Taobao

③然后点击"设置"——"支付宝绑定设置"，如图 22 所示。如果未绑定，请先绑定支付宝账号，下图中的账号是绑定过的，就直接进入下一步。

③You can click the Setting option and choose Alipay Binding as Figure 22 shows. If you have not bound Alipay account，please do the binding process first and move to the next step.

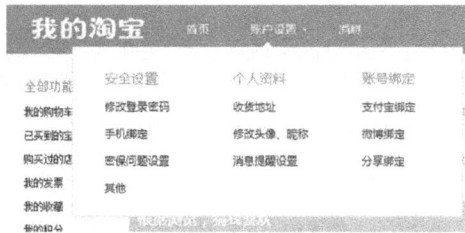

图 22 "支付宝"绑定设置

Figure 22   Setting of Alipay

绑定后的界面如图 23 所示。

The page after the binding is shown as Figure 23.

图 23 "支付宝"绑定成功

Figure 23   Alipay account binding is completed

④然后点击"快捷支付(含卡通)"后面的"查看"链接,就跳转到了支付宝银行卡页面。如图 24 所示,此时可点击"添加银行卡"。

④You can select the Quick Pay option and check the connection, which will link to the Alipay debit/credit cards binding page as Figure 24 shows. Then, you can click the option of "Bank Cards Adding".

图 24 "添加银行卡"界面

Figure 24   Bank Card Adding Page

页面跳转到"关联我的银行卡"页面。如图 25 所示,此时可选择,方式一,通过选择银行发卡行关联;方式二,输入银行卡号关联。

Here comes the page of Connecting to My Bank Cards as Figure 25 shows. Then, there will be two options, the first option is to select the bank and the second option is to enter the card number directly.

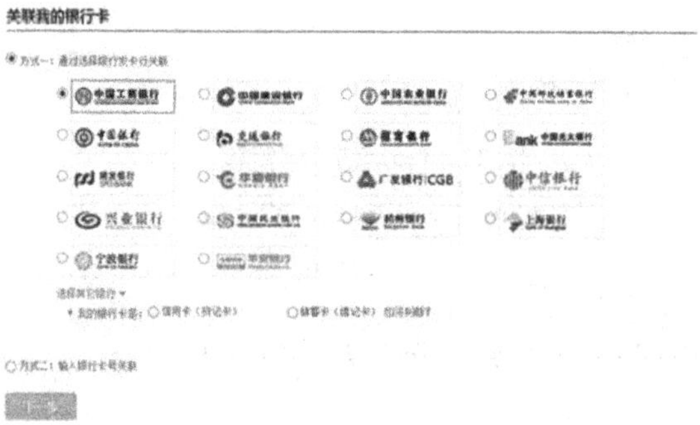

图 25 关联"银行卡"界面

Figure 25   Bank Card Binding Page

若选择方式二,直接输入银行卡号关联。如图 26 所示。

If you choose the second option, you can type in the card's number directly as Figure 26 shows.

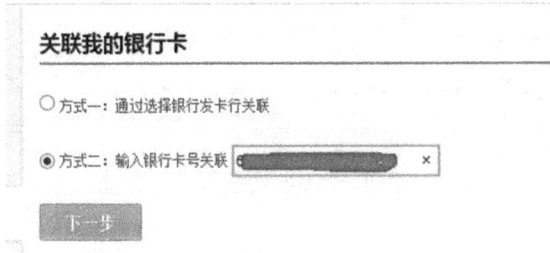

图 26 直接输入卡号关联"银行卡"界面

Figure 26 Bind bank cards by typing in the card's number directly

⑤然后点击"下一步"继续，此时进行简单的设置，然后点击"下一步"。

Click the The Next button and do some simple setting and click the button again.

⑥最后输入手机号、手机号、身份证号等信息，点击"同意协议并开通"，即可完成添加银行卡步骤，如图 27 所示。

You can enter your phone number，ID number and agree to the contracts to finish the card binding process as Figure 27 shows.

图 27 "添加银行卡"成功界面

Figure 27 The Completing Page of Cards Adding

【操作小助手】淘宝网银支付操作流程

[Tips] Taobao Online Banking Payment Process

①进入淘宝网首页，登录你的淘宝账号，然后挑选自己喜欢的商品，如图 28 所示。

You should log into your taobao account first，and then pick your favorite commodities as Figure 28 shows.

图 28　登录淘宝网首页

Figure 28　Logging into Taobao Account

②选购好商品之后,选择加入购物车或立即进行结算,进入订单支付页面。然后确认订单信息,根据提示提交订单,如图 29 到图 31 所示。

After the selecting of commodities，put commodities into carts to check out，then you can place an order as Figure 29 to Figure 31 show.

图 29　选购商品

Figure 29　Selecting Commodities

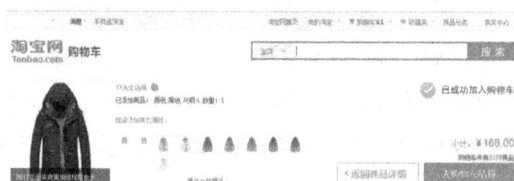

图 30　下单

Figure 30　Checking out

图31 订单结算

Figure 31 Placing the Order

③提交订单后，等待生成一笔未支付的订单。在支付方式中，如果买家需要用支付宝余额支付，请直接安装证书，或者验证手机完成支付，如图32所示。

After the order has been placed，you can do the payment，you can use the money in the Alipay to pay for commodities after the verification as Figure 32 shows.

图32 确认付款

Figure 32 Making Payments

④如果需要与支付宝绑定的网银或者其他网银支付请在其他支付方式中选择银行卡，提交订单（快捷账户安装证书或验证手机直接输入密码即可支付），使用U盾的网银请插入后安装驱动进行支付，如图33所示。

④If you want to pay with bank cards，please select cards option in the payment methods menu（quick-pay users can simply finish the payment by entering passcodes）and use U shield to install drive software to finish the payment as Figure 33 shows.

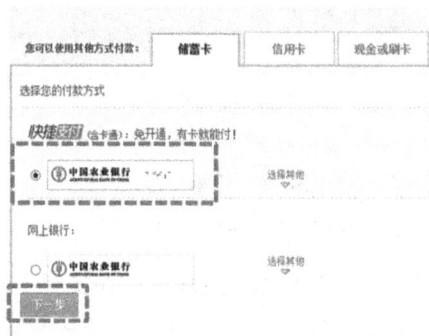

图 33　网银支付

Figure 33　Payment with Online Banking

⑤支付成功,就请坐等收货吧。但是,如果订单出现错误怎么办呢? 这时买家可以进入"我的淘宝"中,查看买到的宝贝,选择"付款",重新进行。

⑤ After the payment has been completed, you can wait for your commodities. If there are some mistakes about the order, buyers can check the commodities they have bought at My Taobao and select the Payment option to redo the order placing process.

【注意事项】信用卡支付手续费

[Notices] Fees for Payments with Credit Cards

买家使用信用卡支付业务购买商品支付宝手续费情况如下。

Buyers using credit cards to pay will have fees occurred.

①使用国际信用卡支付实行相同费率,统一收取交易金额的3%。

①Using international credit cards will have the same fees standard, which is 3% of the transaction amount.

②信用卡分期手续费以支付宝支付页面提示的费率为准。

②Installment payments fees is shown on the paying pages of Alipay.

③所有淘宝集市未开通信用卡支付,但在符合开通信用卡支付资质的类目中,如您无法通过信用卡大额付款,可以选择自己支付交易金额的1%服务费来完成付款。

③All Taobao markets do not support credit cards. But you can pay extra service fees equal to 1% of purchasing amounts to persuade sellers to accept the credit card payments.

④除上述情况外，无须手续费。

④There are no other fees besides the situations shown above.

【操作小助手】亚马逊一键支付操作流程

［Tips］Amazon.com 1-click Ordering Process

①买家进入亚马逊首页（Amazon.com），登录亚马逊的账号，然后挑选自己喜欢的商品，如图34所示。

①Buyers log into their Amazon accounts at the front page of Amazon.com and pick commodities as Figure 34 shows.

图34　选购商品

Figure 34　Choosing Commodities

②选购好商品之后，选择加入购物车或立即进行结算，进入订单支付页面。然后确认订单信息，根据提示提交订单，如图35和图36所示。

Buyers can add commodities to shopping carts and check out. Buyers can place orders step by step as shown in Figure 35 and Figure 36.

图 35　选购商品

Figure 35　Adding Commodities to the Cart

图 36　进入结算中心

Figure 36　Processing to Check-out

　　③买家选择好配送地址和送货方式后,选择支付方式中的"一键信用卡支付"。选择"一键信用卡支付",只需要预先将信用卡信息(银行卡号、持卡人姓名、信用卡有效期)保存到买家亚马逊账户中,如图 37 所示。

　　③Buyers can choose the shipping address and delivery method，and choose credit cards-1-click ordering which requires buyers to save the credit card information upfront（card numbers，cardholders' names，expiring dates）to their amazon accounts as Figure 37 shows.

图 37　信用卡一键支付
Figure 37　Credit Cards 1-click Payment

　　④买家核实所选择的支付方式和其他信息后，点击"订单确认"，完成订单支付，如图 38 所示。

　　④Buyers should double-check the payment method and other information before clicking the Submitting Order button as Figure 38 shows.

图 38　订单确认
Figure 38　Submitting Order

　　⑤下单成功后，包裹发货时，银行会自动从买家的信用卡中扣除相应包裹的金

额,如图 39 所示。

⑤After placing the order, credit cards balance will change after the order has been processed as Figure 39 shows.

图 39　订单成功
Figure 39　Order Placed

【操作小助手】银联在线支付操作流程

[Tips] Payment Process Using Union Pay

①注册开通银行在线支付账户(Account Registering)

在银联网页(www.chinaunionpay.com)首页左下角点击"立即注册"按钮或点击首页右上角的"注册"字样,持卡人都可以进入注册页面,如图 40 所示。

On the left side bottom of the front page of www. chinaunionpay. com, there is an option displaying Register Now. The cardholder can enter the registering page by clicking it as Figure 40 shows.

图 40　"页面欢迎语"界面图
Figure 40　Welcome Page

当持卡人填完所有的信息后，应该阅读并同意用户注册服务协议，点击"提交注册"。

When the cardholder fills the information and agrees to using conditions, the cardholder can click Submit option to complete the registering.

②认证支付（Payment Certification）

第一，在商户网站选择银联在线支付。

Firstly, the user can choose the option of certified payment at the online shopping website.

第二，在支付页面选择"认证支付"，选择持卡人的银联卡类型（信用卡或借记卡）并根据页面输入信息要求输入银行卡号。

Secondly, the user can choose the type of the union pay cards (credit or debit card) and type the card number by the following instructions.

第三，按页面提示，输入有效期、CVN2、短信验证码、校验码，点击"确定支付"。若持卡人发现页面显示的手机号码与持卡人目前使用的手机号码不符时，请先联系持卡人的发卡银行变更"银行预留手机号码"，然后可点击"手机号变更？"再次开通认证支付，如图 41 所示。

Thirdly, following the instruction, the user can type the validity date of cards, CVN2, verification code and identifying code. Then, the user can click Continue Option to complete the payment. If it indicates that the cell phone number is different from the cardholder's, the user can contact the bank to change the reserved number and do above steps one more time as Figure 41 shows.

图 41　银联卡"认证支付"界面图

Figure 41　The Page of Certified Payment

第四,支付成功,如图 42 所示。

Fourthly, the payment has been completed as Figure 42 shows.

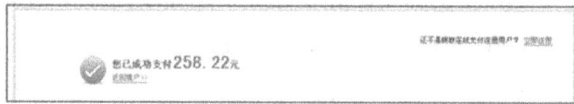

图 42 银联卡"认证支付"确认界面图
Figure 42 The Confirmation Page of Certified Payment

③快捷支付(Quick Pay)

快捷支付是银联为持卡人提供的一种安全便捷的支付方式。注册成为银联在线支付用户并关联银联卡后,持卡人只需输入用户名、登录密码、短信验证码即可完成支付。

Quick pay is a payment method valid for the Union Pay cardholder, which is faster and more convenient. The buyer can register to become a Union Pay user and do the Union Pay payment online by simply entering the username, the passcode and the verification code getting from the text message.

第一,在商户网站选择银联在线支付。

Firstly, the buyer can choose the union pay online option at the merchant website.

第二,在银联在线支付页面,点击"快捷支付"并登录,如图 43 所示。

Secondly, the buyer can choose Quick Pay Option and log into the Union Pay account as Figure 43 shows.

图 43 "快捷支付"登录界面图
Figure 43 The Logging-in Page of Quick Pay

第三,确认用于支付的银行卡号。获取并输入短信验证码,点击"确认支付",如图 44 所示。

Thirdly，the buyer can type in the card number and the verification code and click Confirm option as Figure 44 shows.

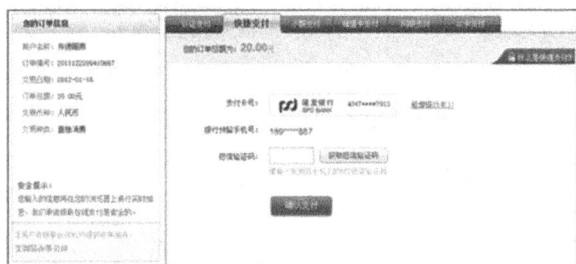

图 44 "快捷支付"操作界面图

Figure 44 The Operation Page of Quick Pay

第四，支付成功，如图 45 所示。

Fourthly，payment has been completed as Figure 45 shows.

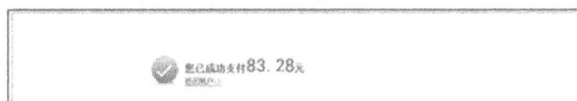

图 45 "快捷支付"提示界面图

Figure 45 The Tips Page of Quick Pay

④小额支付（Micro-Payment）

小额支付是银联为持卡人提供的一种单笔不超过 100 元的便捷支付方式。持卡人在支付时无须短信验证，只要输入银联卡信息（卡号、密码、CVN2 等）即可完成支付。

Micro-Payment provides a convenient way to pay for Union Pay cardholders for consumption amount less than RMB 100. While paying，cardholders can simply enter Union Pay card information（card numbers，passwords，CVN2，etc.）to complete payments without SMS verification.

第一，持卡人用户选择小额支付方式(已开通银联小额支付业务)。

Firstly，the cardholder can select the Micro-Payment method on websites （Union Pay has opened Micro-Payment business）.

第二，选择信用卡或者借记卡支付，并填入银行卡号、有效期、CVN2、校验码，并点击提交，如图 46 所示。

Secondly，the cardholder can choose to pay by credit card or debit card and enter information like the bank card number，the validity，the CVN2 and the check code，and click Submitting Order as Figure 46 shows.

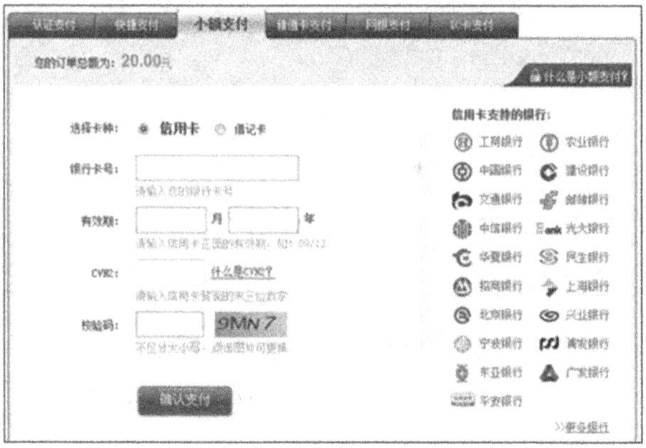

图 46 "小额支付"界面图

Figure 46　The Page of Micro-Payment

第三，页面返回支付成功。

Thirdly，the payment has been completed.

⑤储值卡支付(Stored Value Card Payment)

储值卡支付是指持卡人在银联支付页面上输入储值卡(如中银通卡)卡号、密码即可完成交易的支付方式。储值卡的支付流程如下：

Stored value card payment refers to the cardholder entering the Union Pay card number and the password on the payment page（such as BOC card）to complete the payment process. The stored value card payment process is shown as follows：

第一，在商户网站选择银联在线支付。

Firstly，the buyer can select Union Pay online payment at the merchant website.

第二，选择"储值卡支付"，选择储值卡类型并填入储值卡卡号、密码、校验码，点击"确认支付"，如图 47 所示。

Secondly，the buyer can select the Stored Value Card Payment button to choose the type of stored value cards，and fill in the card number，the password and the verification code，and click Confirm button as Figure 47 shows.

图 47 "储值卡支付"界面图

Figure 47 The Page of Stored Value Card Payment

第三,支付成功。

Thirdly, the payment has been completed.

⑥网银支付（Online Banking Payment）

网银支付的操作流程如下。

Online banking payment operation process is shown as below.

第一,在购物网站选择银联快捷支付。

Firstly, at the online shopping website, the buyer can select Union Pay Quick Pay.

第二,在银联认证支付页面下,点击"网银支付",并输入用于支付的银联卡号,点击"下一步",如图 48 所示。

Secondly, at the Union Pay certification payment page, the buyer can select the Online Banking Payment option, and type the card number and click the Next option as Figure 48 shows.

图 48 "网银支付"登录界面图

Figure 48 The Logging-in Page of Online Banking Payment

第三,在网银页面上,按持卡人银行网银的要求输入相关的支付信息,如图 49 所示。

Thirdly，at the online banking page，the buyer can type in the relevant required payment information as Figure 49 shows.

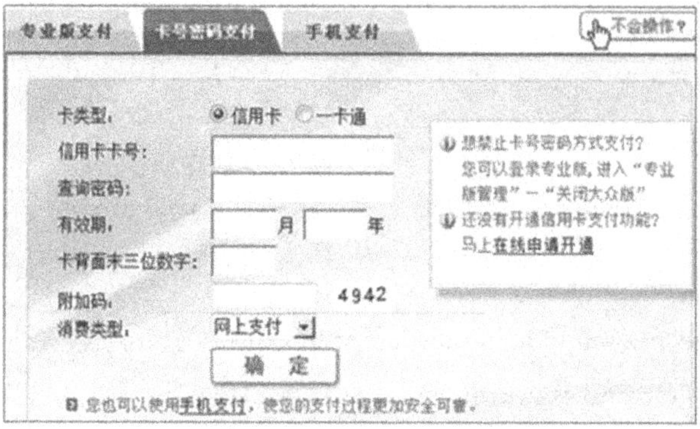

图 49 "网银支付"操作界面图

Figure 49　The Operation Page of Online Banking Payment

第四,支付成功。

Fourthly，the payment has been completed.

3.4 转账支付(Wire Transfer Payment)

概念 (Definition)

转账,是指不直接使用现金,而是通过银行将款项从付款账户划转到收款账户完成货币收付的一种银行货币结算方式。它是随着银行业的发展而逐步发展起来的。当结算金额大、空间距离远时,使用转账结算,可以做到更安全、快速。在现代社会,绝大多数商品交易和货币支付都通过转账结算的方式进行。

Wire transfer refers to money payment transferred from the payer's account to the payee's account to clear the payment. It becomes more and more popular for the development of banking industry. It is much safer and quicker to make settlements by wire transfer payment especially for large amounts and long distance payments. In the modern society，wire transfer does most of the commodity transactions and payments.

支付方式（Payment Methods）

转账结算的方式很多，主要可分为同城结算和异地结算两大类。同城结算包括支票结算、付款委托书结算、同城托收承付结算、托收无承付结算和限额支票结算等；异地结算包括异地托收承付结算、异地委托收款结算、汇兑结算、信用证结算和限额结算等。以下就同城结算中的支票结算和异地结算中的异地委托收款结算方式进行说明。

There are many ways to do the wire transfer settlement，mainly divided into the regional settlement and the remote settlement. The regional settlement includes check clearing，settlement of payment orders，regional collection commitments settlement，collection without acceptance settlement and limit check clearing，etc. Remote settlement includes the remote collection commitments settlement，the nonlocal authorized collection and settlement，the exchange settlement，the letter of credit and the quota settlement，etc. The check clearing in the regional settlement and the nonlocal authorized collection and settlement in the remote settlement will be explained.

（1）支票结算（Check Clearing）

①概念（Definition）

支票结算是指客户根据其所在银行的存款和透支限额开出支票，命令银行从其账户中支付一定款项给受款人，从而实现资金调拨，了结债权债务关系的一种过程。

Check clearing refers to the customer issue checks according to the bank accounts' deposits and credit limit to transfer money from his account to the payee's to do the money transfer to clear debt.

同城票据交换地区的单位、个体户和个人之间的一切款项往来，都可以使用支票。支票分为普通支票、现金支票、转账支票三种。

You can use the check to do the regional bill clearing within individuals and enterprises. Checks can be divided into ordinary check，cash check and wire transfer check.

【小贴士】支票记载事项

[Tips]Check Items

表明"支票"的字样，无条件支付的委托，确定的金额，付款人名称，出票日期，出票人签章。

It should show the word "check" on the bill, unconditional payment entrustment, money amount, name of the payer, the issue date, signature of the issuer.

支票的金额、收款人名称,可以由出票人授权补记,未补记前不得背书转让和提示付款。

The money amount of the check and payee's name can be written afterward by the authorization of the check issuer, the check can not be endorsed or transferred if it is not filled with all the information.

签发支票应使用碳素墨水或墨汁填写,支票的金额、日期、收款人不得更改,其他内容更改,须有出票人加盖预留银行印鉴证明。

The carbon ink or the ink should be used to fill in the check. The money amount, the date and the payee's name shall not be changed. If other contents need to be changed, the bank stamps are required.

②特点(Features)

支票结算的特点概括起来就是简便、灵活、迅速和可靠。

Check clearing's characteristics are simple, flexible, quick and reliable.

第一,简便,是指使用支票办理结算手续简便。只要付款人在银行有足够的存款,它就可以签发支票给收款人,银行凭支票就可以办理款项的划拨或现金的支付。

Firstly, being simple refers that the use of check to do the clearing is simple. As long as the payer has enough deposits, he or she can write a check to the payee. The bank can pay with cash or transfer money from the payer's account to the payee's account.

第二,灵活,是指按照规定,支票可以由付款人向收款人签发以直接办理结算,也可以由付款人出票委托银行主动付款给收款人。另外转账支票在指定的城市中还可以背书转让。

Secondly, being flexible means that the payer can write a check to the payee directly or entrusts a bank to do the payment. In certain areas, wire transfer checks can be endorsed.

第三,迅速,是指使用支票办理结算,收款人将转账支票和进账单送交银行,一般当天或次日即可入账,而使用现金支票当即可取得现金。

Thirdly，being quick refers to that using checks to do the clearing will only take one or two days. You can cash the cash check immediately.

第四，可靠，是指银行严禁签发空头支票，各单位必须在银行存款余额内才能签发支票，因而收款人凭支票就能取得款项，一般是不存在得不到正常支付的情况的。

Fourthly，being reliable refers that banks prohibited the issuance of rubber check，only those with enough deposits can issue a check，so the payee can get their payments. Then，there is little possibility failing to get payment.

③支票操作流程（Process of Check Issuing）

第一，现金支票操作流程（如图 50 所示）。

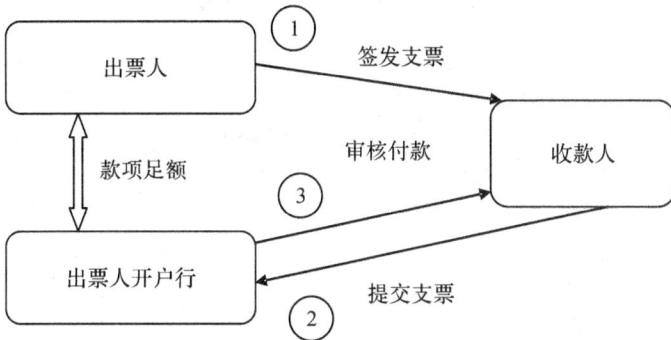

图 50　现金支票操作流程图

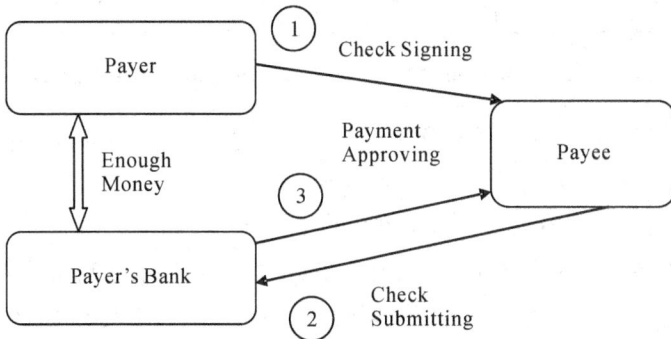

Figure 50　Process of Cash Check Issuing and Cashing

Firstly，process of cash check issuing are shown as Figure 50. 第二，转账支票操作流程（如图 51 所示）。

Secondly，process of wire transfer check issuing and cashing are shown as

Figure 51.

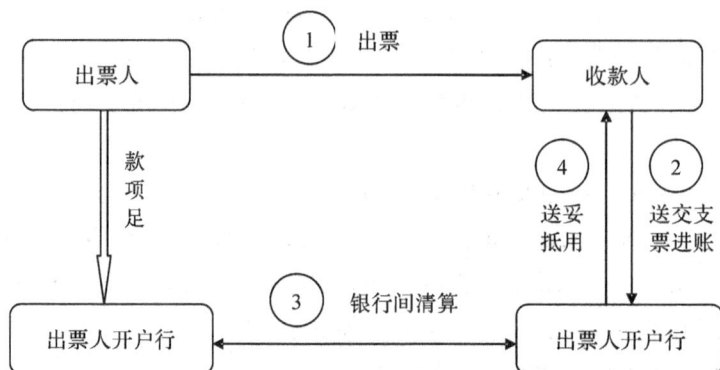

图 51 转账支票操作流程图

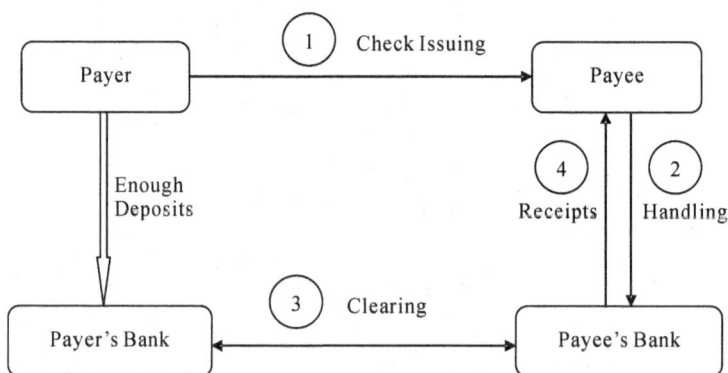

Figure 51 Process of Wire Transfer Checks Issuing and Cashing

【案例链接】空头支票挂失案例

[Case Study]Rubber Check Loss Case

案例过程：宏利天有限责任公司准备购买一批中秋节月饼。9 月 1 日，总经理秘书马瑚女士持一张印章齐全，未填收款单位、金额和日期的现金支票外出采购。马瑚女士在商场选好月饼准备填写支票时，突然发现支票不翼而飞。

Case Process：Honglitian Limited Liability Company was ready to buy a batch of Mid Autumn Festival moon cakes. On September 1，the secretary of the general manager Ms. Ma Hu carried a cash check，which had an integrated stamp but did not have payee's name，the money amount and the date. Miss Ma Hu suddenly found the check was missing while she was selecting moon cakes and was ready to fill in information for the check at the mall.

为防止支票款被冒领，宏利天有限责任公司出具信函，马上派人到开户银行工商银行东铁匠营支行办理了该现金支票的挂失手续。

Honglitian limited Liability Company issued a letter，sent it to ICBC Dongtiejiangying Branch and reported loss of the cash immediately.

9月12日，舞幻汽车维修中心会计持一张现金支票来到工商银行东铁匠营支行要求提取现金。

On September 12，Wuhuan Car Repair Center's accountant came to ICBC Dongtiejiangying Branch to cash a check.

银行经办人员在审查凭证的过程中发现，该支票正是9月1日已做挂失处理的那张支票，遂拒绝付款。

The bank found the check has a loss report during the documents reviewing process，and refused to cash the check.

舞幻汽车维修中心会计提出：该支票是付款单位派人来购买汽车配件时填写的，支票填好后，立即到银行办理提现，不可能在9月1日就将该支票挂失，银行没有理由不予付款。

The accountant said that the check is filled when the buyer came to buy auto parts. They came to ICBC Dongtiejiangying Branch to cash the check right after that；the bank did not have right to refuse.

在银行拿出挂失依据后，舞幻汽车维修中心会计对银行办理挂失提出了异议，认为银行对空白支票不应办理挂失。

After the bank provided the certification for the loss requirement，the accountant said it was not right for the bank to provide loss-reporting service for rubber checks.

银行认为：根据票据法的规定，票据丧失，有确定付款人的票据可以挂失止付。收到挂失止付通知的付款人，应当暂停支付。因此，银行办理挂失是正确的。

The bank said they were doing the right thing according to negotiable instruments law of the People's Republic of China since the check had certain payer and stamps as well.

舞幻汽车维修中心诉至法院，要求银行支付现金50000元。

Wuhuan Car Repair Center filed a lawsuit against ICBC Dongtiejiangying Branch and asked it for cashing for the 50000-worth check.

案例点评:宏利天有限责任公司丢失的支票处于无效状态。丢失的支票无效,宏利天有限责任公司申办挂失,开户银行受理挂失便没有法律依据。工商银行东铁匠营支行对宏利天有限责任公司空白支票的遗失受理挂失是错误的。舞幻汽车维修中心不知支票已丢失的事实,是善意持票人,应该享有票据权利,银行应为其办理提现手续,支票的损失只能由宏利天有限责任公司承担。

Case Review: First of all, the missing check is invalid, and then the loss reporting for an invalid check is improper. Since the car repair center was the weak side and knew nothing about the rubber check, it is suggested the bank cashing the check and making the Honglitian Limited Liability Company take the responsibility.

(2)委托收款结算(Settlement of Entrusted Collection)

①概念(Definition)

委托收款结算是收款人向银行提供收款依据,委托银行向付款人收取款项的一种结算方式。委托收款结算方式是一种建立在商业信用基础上的结算方式,即由收款人先发货或提供劳务,然后通过银行收款,银行不参与监督,结算中发生争议由双方自行协商解决。因此收款单位在选用此种结算方式时应当慎重,应当了解付款方的资信状况,以免发货或提供劳务后不能及时收回款项。

Settlement of entrusted collection is the payment that the payee provides documents and entrusts the bank to collect the money. It is a kind of payments that is based on the business asking the payee to send the goods or provide the services first before he or she entrusts the bank to collect the money for them without supervision, the disputes occurring during the settlement should be dealt by negotiation done by both parties. Therefore, the payee is supposed to choose this payment method carefully and try to know the credit status of the payer to avoid a loss or a delay.

单位和个人凭债券、存单、已承兑的商业汇票等付款人的债务证明办理款项的结算,均可以使用委托收款结算方式。

Entities and individuals may choose settlement of collection to collect payment from debt certification such as bonds, certificate of deposits and accepted commercial bills, etc.

委托收款在同城、异地均可以使用。委托收款结算款项的划回方式,分邮寄和电报两种,由收款人选用。

Entrusted collection of payment can be used both locally and remotely. The payee can choose either mail or telegram to delimit the payment.

【小贴士】委托收款凭证记载事项

[Tips]Required Items for Certificates for Entrusted Collections of Payment

表明“托收”的字样，确定的金额，付款人名称，收款人名称，委托收款凭据名称及附寄单证张数，托收日期，收款人签章。欠缺记载上列事项之一的，银行不予受理。托收凭证如图 52 所示。

The word “collection”, the money amount determined, the payers’ name, the payee’s name, the name of certificate for entrusted collections of payment and the sheets number of enclosed documents, the collection date and the payee’s signature are needed. The bank will not accept the certificates if one of the items listed above lacks. The certificates for entrusted collections are shown as Figure 52.

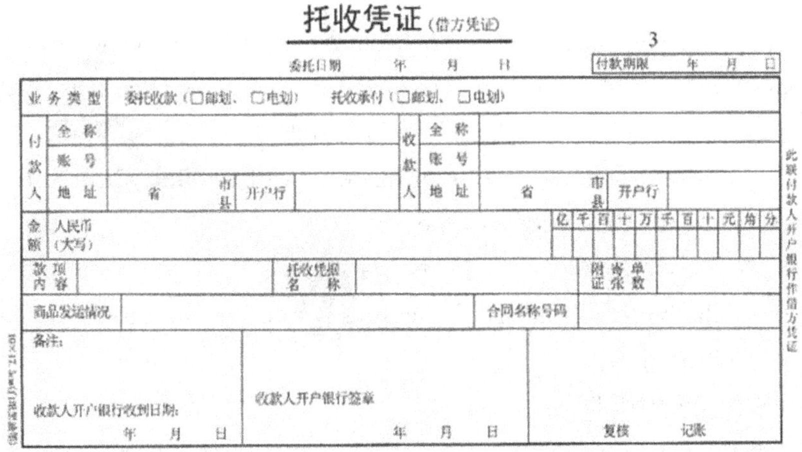
托收凭证（借方凭证）

3

委托日期 年 月 日 | 付款期限 年 月 日

业务类型	委托收款（□邮划、□电划） 托收承付（□邮划、□电划）						
付款人	全称			收款人	全称		
	账号				账号		
	地址	省 市县	开户行		地址	省 市县	开户行
金额	人民币（大写）				亿 千 百 十 万 千 百 十 元 角 分		
款项内容		托收凭据名称		附寄单证张数			
商品发运情况				合同名称号码			
备注： 收款人开户银行收到日期： 年 月 日		收款人开户银行签章 年 月 日		复核 记账			

此联付款人开户银行作借方凭证

图 52 托收凭证样图

Figure 52 A Sample of Certificates for Entrusted Collections of Payment

②特点(Features)

委托收款具有使用范围广、灵活、简便等特点。

The entrusted collection of payment can be used within wide areas and is simple and flexible, etc.

第一，从使用范围来看，凡是商品交易、劳务款项及其他应收款项的结算都可以使用委托收款结算方式。城镇公用企事业单位向用户收取的水费、电费、电话费、邮费、煤气费等也都可以采用委托收款结算方式。

Firstly，the entrusted collection will be a good way to do money transaction occurred during shopping，salaries paying and receivables collection. Electricity bills，water bills，phone bills，mailing bills and gas bills can be collected with the entrusted collection method as well.

第二，委托收款不受金额起点的限制。凡是收款单位发生的各种应收款项，不论金额大小，只要委托银行就给办理。

Secondly，the entrusted collection of payment is not limited by the money amount. As far as the entrustment has been requested，the bank should accept it.

第三，委托收款不受地点的限制，在同城、异地都可以办理。

Thirdly，entrusted collection of payment is not limited by the area，and can be done regionally and remotely.

第四，委托收款有邮寄和电报划回两种方式，收款单位可以根据需要进行灵活选择。

Fourthly，the entrusted collection of payment can be done in two ways，which are mailing and telegraphic transfer. The payee can choose between these two.

第五，委托收款付款期为三天，凭证索回期为两天。

Fifthly，the entrusted collection of payment will be done within three days，receipts will be sent back within two days.

第六，银行不负责审查付款单位拒付理由。

Sixthly，the bank will not check reasons if payers refuse to pay.

③流程（Procedures）

委托收款流程如图 53 所示。

The settlement of entrusted collection of payment is processed as below.

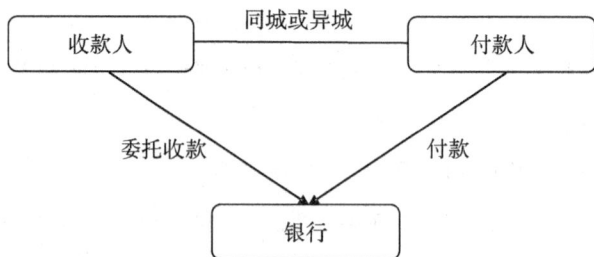

图 53　委托收款流程图

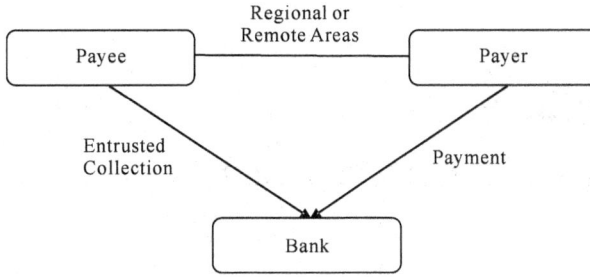

Figure 53 Process of Entrusted Collection of Payment

4 机构解密
（Institution Decoding）

4.0 导言 （Introduction）

金融机构，是指专门从事货币信用活动的中介组织。我国的金融机构，按地位和功能可分为四大类。第一类，中央银行，即中国人民银行。第二类，银行，包括政策性银行、商业银行、村镇银行。第三类，非银行金融机构，主要包括国有及股份制的保险公司、城市信用合作社、证券公司（投资银行）、财务公司等。第四类，在境内开办的外资、侨资、中外合资金融机构。以上各种金融机构相互补充，构成了一个完整的金融机构体系。

Financial institutions are the intermediaries specializing in the activities of money credits. The financial institutions in China can be sorted into four types according to their importance and functions：①central bank，namely，the People's Bank of China；②banks including policy banks，commercial banks and rural banks；③non-bank financial institutions，mainly including state-owned and commercial insurance companies，rural credit cooperatives，securities（investment banks）and finance companies；④financial institutions of foreign funds，overseas funds and Sino-foreign joint-venture banks in China. All the above-mentioned institutions constitute a complete financial system by mutual complement.

4.1 中央银行（Central Bank）

中央银行是一国最高的货币金融管理机构，在各国金融体系中居于主导地位。中央银行的职能是由中央银行的性质决定的，同时也是中央银行性质的具体体现。其职能主要是宏观调控、保障金融安全与稳定、金融服务。

Being the supreme regulatory agency of a country's money and finance, the central bank predominates in the financial system of the country. The functions of central bank is determined and also embodied by its features. Generally speaking, central bank mainly bears the functions as macro control, financial security and stability as well as financial services.

中央银行是"发行货币的银行"，对调节货币供应量、稳定币值有重要作用。中央银行是"银行的银行"，它集中保管银行的准备金，并对它们发放贷款，充当"最后贷款者"。

Central bank is the bank issuing banknotes and playing an important role in adjusting money supply and stabilizing the currency value. Besides, central bank is also the "Bank of Banks" which safeguards the banks' reserves collectively and makes loans to banks as lender of last resort.

中央银行是"国家的银行"，它是国家货币政策的制定者和执行者，也是政府干预经济的工具；同时为国家提供金融服务，代理国库，代理发行政府债券，为政府筹集资金，代表政府参加国际金融组织和各种国际金融活动。

Central bank is the bank of one country, acting as the framer and performer of monetary policy, and the instrument of the government to intervene the economy. It also provides financial services for its country, acts as fiscal agent, issues government securities as agent, raises funds for the government and takes part in different international financial organizations and activities on behalf of the government.

中央银行的主要业务有货币发行、集中存款准备金、贷款、再贴现、证券、黄金占款和外汇占款、为商业银行和其他金融机构办理资金的划拨清算和资金转移等。

Central bank's main businesses are as follows: issuing currency, concentrating required reserves, loans, rediscounts, securities, position for bullion purchase and funds outstanding for foreign exchange, transacting the businesses of fund transfer, payment and remittance for commercial banks and other financial institutions.

中央银行所从事的业务与其他金融机构所从事的业务的根本区别在于，中央银行所从事的业务不是为了营利，而是为了实现国家宏观经济目标服务，这是由中央银行所处的地位和性质决定的。

The basic difference between the businesses carried by the central bank and other financial institutions lies in central bank's non-profit purpose but serving the realization of national macroeconomic target, which is decided by the position and features of central bank.

世界上最早成立的中央银行，是瑞典国家银行和英格兰银行。瑞典国家银行的前身是 1656 年由私人创办的欧洲第一家发行银行券的银行，于 1668 年由政府出面改组为国家银行，对国会负责。英格兰银行是 1694 年根据《国王特准法》设立的私人股份银行，它独享货币发行特权，比瑞典国家银行早 53 年。

The earliest central banks in the world were the Sveriges Riksbank and the Bank of England. The predecessor of Sveriges Riksbank was a private European bank set up in 1656 which was the first bank to issue banknotes; it was reorganized to a national bank in 1668 by the government and was responsible for the Congress. The Bank of England was a private joint-stock bank set up in 1694 according to the *Monarchy Law*, it has a monopoly on the issue of banknotes and was set up 53 years earlier than the Sveriges Riksbank.

中国人民银行（The People's Bank of China）

中国人民银行于 1948 年 12 月 1 日在华北银行、北海银行、西北农民银行的基础上合并组成。

The People's Bank of China was set up on December 1, 1948, based on the combination of the Huabei Bank, the Beihai Bank and the Xibei Farmer Bank.

西北农民银行壹圆纸币
（One-yuan Banknote of the Xibei Farmer Bank）

1983 年，国务院决定由中国人民银行专门行使国家中央银行职能。职能含金融风险防范与化解、统计数据、银行卡、金融规章、反假货币工作、公告栏等。

The People's Bank of China was authorized by the State Council in 1983 to act as central bank with functions including precautions against and defusion of financial risks, statistical data, credit cards, financial regulations, anti-counterfeit work and bulletin, etc.

中国人民银行是中华人民共和国的中央银行，是中华人民共和国国务院组成部门之一。中国人民银行根据《中华人民共和国中国人民银行法》（下面简称《中国人民银行法》）的规定，在国务院的领导下依法独立执行货币政策，履行职责，开展业务，不受地方政府、各级政府部门、社会团体和个人的干涉。《中国人民银行法》对我国中国人民银行的性质及法律地位做了明确规定。

The People's Bank of China is the central bank of the People's Republic of China and an important organ of the State Council. Under the leadership of the State Council, it independently carries out monetary policy, executes duties and conducts businesses beyond the interference from local governments, governmental departments of different levels, social entities and individuals according to the regulations in *Law of the People's Bank of China* which also explicitly stipulates the characteristics and legal position of the People's Bank of China as follows.

（1）中国人民银行是中华人民共和国的中央银行。中国人民银行在国务院的领导下，制定和实施货币政策，防范和化解金融风险，维护金融稳定。

（1）The People's Bank of China is the central bank of the People's Republic of China. It shall perform the functions to make and implement monetary policy, precaution against and defuse financial risks and maintain the financial stability.

（2）中国人民银行应当向全国人民代表大会常务委员会提出有关货币政策情况和金融监管情况的工作报告。

（2）The People's Bank of China shall put forward the matters about monetary policy and the working report of financial supervision.

（3）中国人民银行就年度货币供应量、利率、汇率和国务院规定的其他重要事项做出的决定，报国务院批准后执行。中国人民银行就其他有关货币政策事项做出决定后，即予执行，并报国务院备案。

（3）The People's Bank of China shall present the State Council for the approval of the decisions on annual quantity supplied of money，interest rates，exchange rates and other important matters stipulated by the State Council. Other matters related to monetary policy can be carried out at once after the decision of the People's Bank of China with the report to the State Council for record.

（4）中国人民银行在国务院的领导下依法独立执行货币政策，履行职责，开展业务，不受地方政府、各级政府部门、社会团体和个人的干涉，具有相对独立性。

（4）Under the leadership of the State Council，the People's Bank of China enjoys relative independence in carrying out monetary policy，executes duties and conducts businesses beyond the interference from local governments，governmental departments of different levels，social entities and individuals.

（5）中国人民银行实行行长负责制。行长的人选，根据国务院总理的提名，由全国人民代表大会决定；全国人民代表大会闭会期间，由全国人民代表大会常务委员会决定，由中华人民共和国主席任免；副行长由国务院总理任免。

（5）The People's Bank of China shall practice a system wherein the Governor shall assume overall responsibility. The candidate for central bank governor is nominated by the prime minister of the State Council and decided by the National People's Congress（NPC）；the candidate shall be decided by the Standing Committee of the NPC when it is not in session；the appoint and dismiss of governor of bank is up to the president while those of the deputy-governor are up to the prime minister of the State Council.

（6）中国人民银行实行独立的财务预算管理制度。但应当执行法律、行政法规和国家统一的财务会计制度，并接受国务院审计机关和财政部门依法分别进行的审计和监督。

(6) The People's Bank of China shall implement financial budget control system but it shall also carry out the laws, executive regulations as well as the unified financial and accounting systems of the country. It shall be audited and supervised respectively by the auditing agency and financial sector of the State Council.

英格兰银行(The Bank of England)

英格兰银行,成立于 1694 年,是英国的中央银行,也是世界上最早形成的中央银行,为各国中央银行体制的鼻祖。它负责召开货币政策委员会,对英国国家的货币政策负责。英格兰银行总部大楼位于伦敦的主要金融区——伦敦市的针线大街,因此它有时候又被人称为"针线大街上的老妇人"或者"老妇人"。英格兰银行自 1694 年成立以来一直是一家私营银行,直到 1946 年收归国有。1998 年英格兰银行成为一个独立的公共机构,由代表政府的财政部全资律师负责,享有制定货币政策的独立性。

The Bank of England is the central bank of the United Kingdom and the model on which most modern central banks have been based. Established in 1694, it is one of the oldest central banks in the world. It is responsible for convening Monetary Policy Committee (MPC) and the national monetary policy of the United Kingdom. The Bank's headquarters is located at the Threadneedle Street in London's main financial district. Therefore, it is sometimes known by the metonym The Old Lady of Thread Needle Street or The Old Lady. The bank was privately owned from its foundation in 1694 until nationalized in 1946. In 1998, it became an independent public organization, wholly owned by the Treasury Solicitor on behalf of the government, with independence in setting monetary policy.

英格兰银行是英国八家授权发行货币的银行之一,享有在英格兰、威尔士发钞的特权,苏格兰和北爱尔兰由一般商业银行发钞,但以英格兰发行的钞票做准备;作为银行的最后贷款人,保管商业银行的存款准备金,并作为票据的结算银行,对英国的商业银行及其他金融机构进行监管;作为政府的银行,代理国库,稳定英镑币值及代表政府参加一切国际性财政金融机构。因此,英格兰银行具有典型的中央银行的"发行的银行""银行的银行""政府的银行"的特点。

The Bank of England is one of eight banks authorized to issue banknotes in the United Kingdom，but has a monopoly on the issue of banknotes in England and Wales and regulates the issue of banknotes by commercial banks in Scotland and Northern Ireland. As a bank lender of last resort，the bank takes care of required reserves of commercial banks；meanwhile，as a clearing bank，it regulates the commercial banks and other financial institutions in the UK. As the government's bank，the Bank of England acts as the agency of national treasury，stabilizing the value of Pound and participating in all international financial institutions on behalf of the government. As a result，the Bank of England has all the features of a typical central bank：bank of issuing, bank of banks and bank of government.

美国联邦储备银行(Federal Reserve Bank)

美国联邦储备银行，位于自由大道33号，于1914年11月由美国众议院所通过成立，以协助联储会监理银行与金融。美国联邦储备银行是世界上最具实力的银行，是世界上美元和黄金最多的地方。实际上包括12家银行及其分布在全美各地的25家地区分行，每个银行分管自己的联邦储备辖区。尽管它最初设立目的是稳定和保护美国的银行系统，但其目前的主要职责却是控制通货膨胀。

It is located in 33 Freedom Avenue，the Federal Reserve Bank was founded by Congress in November，1914 to cooperate with committee to monitor banking and finance. The Federal Reserve Bank is the most powerful bank in the world，holding the largest amount of US Dollars and gold. Actually，the Federal Reserve Bank System consists of 12 banks and 25 regional branches and each bank takes charge of its federal reserve district. The main role of the Federal Reserve Bank is to control inflation，although it also provides the nation with a safer，more flexible，and more stable monetary and financial system.

美联储是美国的中央银行，其货币政策和公布的数据对经济预测、监管银行机构、稳定金融体系和对外汇与外贸市场有巨大影响。

The Federal Reserve Bank as the central bank of USA，sets the nation's monetary policy，publishes economic data and forecast economy，supervises and regulates banking institutions，maintains the stability of the financial system，and conducts foreign exchange and foreign market.

根据美国联邦储备银行的章程，它的宗旨是"帮助消除通货膨胀和通货紧缩的影响，并积极参与创造环境，促进高就业率、稳定物价、国民经济增长和不断提升的消费水平"。美国联邦储备银行的另一项重要职责是推动资金在银行系统内安全高效地流转。

As set forth in the *Federal Reserve Act*, the Federal Reserve System's aims include promoting maximum employment and economic growth, stablizing prices, moderating long-term interest rates, encouraging consumption. The Federal Reserve performs an important function by promoting a safe, efficient, and accessible system for US Dollars transactions.

美联储由一个 7 人组成的总裁委员会负责管理，所有委员均由总裁予以委任。每个委员的任期长达 14 年。总裁委员会下设一名主席和一名副主席，其任期均为 4 年。由 12 名委员组成的联邦公开市场委员会（FOMC）则是一个具有重要影响力的组织，该委员会每年召开 8 次会议，研讨美国的经济和货币政策。简而言之，掌控世界经济的美国经济，尽在美国联邦储备银行的掌控之中。

It is run by seven members who are nominated by the President of the United States and confirmed in their positions by the US Senate. Each member of the Board of Governors is appointed for a 14-year term. The Chairman and Vice Chairman of the Board are also appointed by the President and confirmed by the Senate, but serve only four-year terms. The FOMC has 8 meetings annually and makes all decisions regarding the conduct of open market operations. The FOMC is charged with overseeing "open market operations", the principal tool by which the Federal Reserve executes US monetary policy. In short, Fed takes charge of US economy which takes charge of the world economy.

欧洲中央银行（European Central Bank，ECB）

欧洲中央银行，简称"欧洲央行"，总部位于德国法兰克福，负责欧盟欧元区的金融及货币政策。欧洲中央银行是根据 1992 年《马斯特里赫特约》的规定于 1998 年 7 月 1 日正式成立的，是为了适应欧元发行流通而设立的金融机构，同时也是欧洲经济一体化的产物。

The ECB, founded in Frankfurt am Main, Germany in July 1, 1998, is an official EU institution at the heart of the Eurosystem and the Single Supervisory

Mechanism. As set forth: in the *Treaty of Maastricht* (1992), its establishment conforms to euro issuance and circulation, and is the product of European Economic Integration.

　　首任欧洲中央银行行长为维姆·德伊森贝赫,荷兰人,曾任荷兰央行行长,曾在阿姆斯特丹大学教授宏观经济学。其继任人为让-克洛德·特里谢,法国人,曾任法国央行法兰西银行行长,于 2003 年 11 月接任。现任欧洲中央银行行长为马里奥·德拉基,意大利人,曾任意大利银行行长,于 2011 年 11 月接任。

The ECB's first president was Win Duisenberg from Holland, previous president of Central Bank of Holland and previous macroeconomics professor of University of Amsterdam. Jean-Claude Trichet became his successor in November, 2003, who had been president of Central bank of France. Mario Draghi, an Italian, has become the ECB's President since November, 2011, who was President of Bank of Italy.

　　欧洲中央银行是世界上第一个管理超国家货币的中央银行。独立性是它的一个显著特点,它接受欧盟领导机构的指令,不受各国政府的监督。它是唯一有资格允许在欧盟内部发行欧元的机构。1999 年 1 月 1 日欧元正式启动后,11 个欧元国政府失去了制定货币政策的权力,必须实行欧洲中央银行制定的货币政策。

The ECB is the first central bank to supervise a regional currency. The independence of the ECB is conducive to maintaining price stability. Neither the ECB nor the national central banks, nor any member of their decision-making bodies, are allowed to seek or take instructions from the EU institutions or bodies, from any government of an EU member state or from any other body. It has exclusive privilege to issue euro in the EU. The euro was launched on January 1, 1999. Since then, 11 member states of the euro area have lost their right to make monetary policies and instead carried out the ECB's monetary policy.

　　欧洲中央银行的组织机构主要包括执行董事会、欧洲央行委员会和扩大委员会。执行董事会由行长、副行长和 4 名董事组成,负责欧洲央行的日常工作;由执行董事会和 12 个欧元国的央行行长共同组成的欧洲央行委员会,是负责确定货币政策和保持欧元区内货币稳定的决定性机构;欧洲央行扩大委员会由央行行长、副行长及欧盟所有 12 国的央行行长组成,其任务是保持欧盟中欧元国家与非欧元国家接触。

The ECB's organization includes the Executive Board, Governing Council and

General Council. The Executive Board consists of president, vice-president and four other members, responsible for daily affairs. The Governing Council is the main decision-making body of the ECB. It consists of the six members of the Executive Board, plus the governors of the national central banks of the twelve euro area countries. It is responsible to make monetary policy and to maintain price stability. The General Council comprises president of the ECB, vice-president of the ECB and governors of the national central banks of the 12 EU member states. It is responsible to keep contact between euro-zone countries and non-euro-zone countries within the Euro.

4.2 商业银行(Commercial Banks)

商业银行是以追求利润最大化为经营目标，以多种金融负债筹集资金，多种金融资产为经营对象。商业银行在国民经济生活中发挥着四大职能，分别是信用中介职能、支付中介职能、信用创造职能、金融服务职能。主要的组织制度包括单一银行制、分支行制、银行控股公司制、连锁银行制。

Commercial banks' operating goal is to maximize profits. They raise funds using financial liabilities and make profits out of financial assets. Commercial banks have four main functions, which are credit intermediary, settlement intermediary, credit creation and financial services. The organization systems of commercial banks include unit banking system, branches system, banking holding company system and chain banking system.

商业银行虽然业务主要集中在经营存款和贷款（放款）业务，即以较低的利率借入存款，以较高的利率放出贷款，存贷款之间的利差就是商业银行的主要利润，但是依然具有多种多样的业务范围，可分为负债业务、资产业务、中间业务。负债业务是形成商业银行资金来源的业务，包括自由资本、存款和借款。资产业务是商业银行将其通过负债业务所聚集的货币资金加以运用的业务，是获得收益的主要业务，包括现金资产、贷款业务和证券投资业务。中间业务是指商业银行不用或较少使用资金，以中间人身份代客户办理收付和其他委托事项而收取手续费的业务，包括结算业务、代理业务、银行卡业务、信托业务、租赁业务和信息咨询业务。

Commercial banks are one type of financial institutions that mainly provide services as accepting deposits, making business loans and offering basic investment products. However, they do have services more that those, which can be divided as liabilities business, assets business and intermediary business. Liabilities business are funds raising business, which includes capital business, deposits business and borrowing business. Assets business are profits earning business, which includes cash items business, loans business and securities business. Intermediary business does not occupy commercial banks' funds that much, which means commercial banks will behave like brokers on behalf of customers and charge services fee. Intermediary business includes settlement business, agency business, bank card business, trust business, leasing business and information consulting business.

商业银行经营管理的基本原则包括安全性原则、流动性原则和营利性原则,通过协调这三个原则,保证商业银行经营活动正常有效地进行。商业银行的监管指标包括不良贷款比例、流动性比例、资本充足率、资本净额、净利润、资产利润率、资本利润率等。

Commercial banks operate under three principles, which are security, liquidity and profitability. Through the coordination of these three principles, commercial banks ensure the effective operating of normal business activities. Regulatory indicators of commercial banks include non-performing loans ratio, liquidity ratio, capital adequacy ratio, net capital, net profit, return on assets, return on equity.

美国花旗银行(Citibank, N. A.)

花旗集团是当今世界资产规模最大、利润最多、全球连锁性最高、业务门类最齐全的金融服务集团。花旗银行是 1955 年由纽约花旗银行与纽约第一国民银行合并而成的,合并后改名为纽约第一花旗银行,1962 年改为第一花旗银行,1976 年3 月 1 日改为现名。花旗集团是世界上规模最大的全能金融集团之一。

Citigroup is a financial service group with the largest assets scale, the most profitable, the highest global chain and the most complete in its businesses in the world. The Citibank was the result of the merger of Citibank, New York and the first national bank, New York and hereafter changed name into the First Citibank, New York in 1955, then into the First Citibank in 1962, it got the present name of Citigroup on March 1, 1976. Citigroup is one of the largest all-round financial groups in the world.

花旗集团的历史可追溯到当时数家从事金融服务业的机构。首先是 1812 年于美国成立的纽约城市银行，由斯提耳曼家族创立，经营与拉丁美洲贸易有关的金融业务，是贸易融资的先驱。1865 年，该行取得国民银行执照，改为纽约花旗银行。集团其他公司主要的前身是 1873 年 Charles D. Barney 在费城成立的证券经纪公司，以及 1892 年 Edward B. Smith 在费城成立的一家证券公司。

The history of Citigroup can be traced back to several financial service institutions at that time. First was City Bank of New York in 1812, which was set up by Stilman family who managed financial businesses related to Latin American trade and was the pioneer of trade financing. In 1865, it gained the bank charter of National Bank and changed into Citibank, New York. The other main predecessors of the group's companies were security brokerage firm established by Charles D. Barney in Philadelphia in 1873 and one security company set up by Edward B. Smith in Philadelphia in 1892.

汇丰集团(HSBC)

汇丰银行由苏格兰人托玛斯·萨瑟兰德于 1864 年在香港发起，资本 500 万港元。最初担任发起委员会成员的包括宝顺洋行、琼记洋行、沙逊洋行、大英轮船、禅臣、太平洋行、顺章洋行等十家洋行。汇丰集团是由香港上海汇丰银行经多年扩展而成。香港上海汇丰银行于 1865 年 3 月在香港开业，同年于上海及伦敦开设分行，又在旧金山设立代理行，其成立的原因是香港洋行的权力划分。

HSBC (Hong Kong and Shanghai Banking Corporation) was first launched by a Scottish named Thomas Sutherland in 1864 with capital of five million Hong kong Dollars. The original committee members hold the post of sponsor were ten foreign firms including Messrs Dent & Co. (Chairman of the committee), Messrs Aug Heard & Co, Messrs Sassoon Sons & Co, The Peninsular & Oriental Steam, Messrs Siemssen & Co, Gilman & Co. and Messr P Cama Co., etc. HSBC had been gradually extended from Hong Kong and Shanghai Banking Corporation for many years. Hong Kong and Shanghai Banking Corporation (HSBC) first started its businesses in March, 1865. The establishment of its Shanghai and London branches and its corresponding bank in San Francisco in the same year stemmed from the division of powers of Hong

Kong's froeign firms.

汇丰银行自 1865 年在上海开业以来,内地的业务从未间断,尤其擅长贸易融资。个人业务范围也不断扩大。随着中国加入世界贸易组织后金融市场的不断开放,汇丰在内地的服务范围也迅速扩大,以满足客户在中国市场的需求。1997 年,汇丰银行成为首批在上海浦东经营人民币业务的外资银行之一;1998 年,汇丰银行更率先成为全国人民币同类拆借市场一级成员,并获准通过该市场进行人民币债券和回购买卖。汇丰银行(中国)有限公司于 2007 年 4 月 2 日正式开业,总行设于上海,是香港上海汇丰银行有限公司全资拥有的银行,其前身是香港上海汇丰银行有限公司的原中国内地分支机构。

HSBC, especially good at trade financing, has never interrupted its businesses in Chinese mainland since it was opened in Shanghai in 1865. With the constant openness of Chinese financial market to the world after the entry to WTO, HSBC quickly expended it business scope in mainland to meet the requirements of clients in Chinese market. HSBC was one of foreign banks who can first engage in RMB business in Pudong District of Shanghai in 1997, and it also took the lead in becoming the primary member of national RMB inter-bank lending market in 1998 and was allowed to deal RMB bonds and repurchases. HSBC (China) headquarted in Shanghai, officially started business on April 2, 2007. It was a wholly funded bank by Hong Kong and Shanghai Banking Corporation Limited, whose predecessor was the original mainland branches.

目前,汇丰中国共有近 150 个网点,汇丰是在内地投资最多的银行之一,入股内地中资金融机构及自身发展的总投资已超过 50 亿美元,其中包括入股上海银行 8% 的股份,平安保险 16.8% 的股份,以及交通银行 19% 的股份。

Having almost one hundred and fifty outlets in mainland, HSBC (China) is one of the banks who invest most in Chinese mainland with a total investment more than 5 billion US Dollars in Chinese institutions and its own development, among which includes 8 percent of shares in Bank of Shanghai, 16.8 percent of shares in Ping An Insurance, and 19 percent of shares in Bank of Communications, etc.

2014 年 2 月 21 日,汇丰中国宣布,已开始协助法国圣戈班集团通过其下属一家上海自贸试验区内的子公司开展跨境人民币经常项目集中收付业务,包括代收代付和净额结算,由此成为首批为上海自贸区企业开展此类业务的银行。这是汇丰中国在 2014 年推出上海自贸区跨境人民币资金池业务后的又一重要业务创新，也体现了银行在运用金融创新支持实体经济方面的一个重要进展。

HSBC（China） announced to assist Saint-Gobain Group （France） in carrying out Cross-border RMB current account collection businesses including export & import collection and net settlement by means of subsidiary cooperation of Saint-Gobain Group （France） in Shanghai Free Trade Zone on February 21，2014，thus becoming one of the banks which first conduct businesses in the Free Trade Zone. Carrying-out of such kind of business was another business innovation of HSBC（China）after its detrusion of Cross-border RMB capital pool in Shanghai Free Trade Zone in 2014，reflecting HSBC's important progress in applying financial innovation to the real economy.

浙商银行（China Zheshang Bank，CZB）

浙商银行是经中国银监会批准设立的全国性股份制商业银行，全称为"浙商银行股份有限公司"。它是一家于 1993 年在宁波成立的中外合资银行；2004 年 6 月 30 日，经中国银监会批准、重组、更名、迁址，改制为现在的浙商银行，并于 2004 年 8 月 18 日正式开业，注册资本 100 亿元，总行设在浙江省杭州市。浙商银行标志以玉琮与算盘为基本元素设计而成，融合稳健与灵动、儒雅与严谨、明礼与诚信、雍容与节俭，彰显浙商银行传承深厚的历史文化，继往开来、求实创新的理念。

China Zheshang Bank is an national commercial bank，which is also known as "CZB". It was originally established in 1993 as a joint venture bank in Ningbo. On June 30，2004，approved by the China Banking Regulatory Commission，it restructured，renamed，changed location and reopened on August 18，2004 and headquartered in Hangzhou. The new China Zheshang Bank has registered capital of RMB 10 Billion Yuan. The sign of China Zheshang Bank is the combination of jade and abacus，which means China Zheshang Bank has the quality of reliability and smartness，elegance and rigorousness，courtesy and honesty，grace and frugality. China Zheshang Bank inherits Zhejiang culture and Zhejiang spirit，which makes it has both realistic and innovative ideas.

浙商银行发展总目标为"两最"：也就是到 2025 年左右，成为最具竞争力的全国性股份制商业银行和浙江省最重要的金融平台。市场和业务定位为"一体两翼",也就是以公司业务为主体,以小企业银行和投资银行业务为两翼。浙商银行目前已在北京、天津、上海、辽宁、江苏、山东、广东、重庆、四川、陕西、甘肃 11 个省市和浙江省内全部省辖市设立了 130 余家机构,全国性机构体系初步形成。

The development objectives of China Zheshang Bank are to become the most competitive national commercial bank and the most important financial platform in Zhejiang. The marketing orientation of China Zheshang Bank has "One Body and Two Wings", which means it takes corporation banking business as the most important business and take small business banking and investment banking business as the two main assistant businesses to maintain the development of the bank. Now, China Zheshang Bank has over 130 branches in Beijing, Tianjin, Liaoning Province, Shanghai, Jiangsu Province, Shandong Province, Sichuan Province, Gansu Province, Chongqing, Shanxi Province, and all cities in Zhejiang Province, which makes it a national commercial bank.

浙商银行在资产负债管理上走轻资产和效益型路线,已经具有发展优势和喜人成绩。2015 年年底,浙商银行总资产达 10316.5 亿元,全年营业收入为 251.3 亿元,同比增长 44.45%,拨备前利润 168.73 亿,净利润 70.51 亿元,增幅分别达 48.42%、38.37%。不良贷款余额 42.33 亿元,不良贷款率 1.23%,拨备覆盖率 240.83%,优于同业平均水平;贷款拨备率 2.95%,比上年提高 0.36 百分点。

China Zheshang Bank takes asset-light and profit-oriented strategy, which helps it develop. At the end of 2015, the total asset of China Zheshang Bank was RMB 1.03165 trillion Yuan. The annual revenue was RMB 25.13 billion which was an increase of 44.45% from a year ago. The pre-provision profit was RMB 16.873 billion Yuan and the net profit was RMB 7.051 billion, with an increase of 48.42% and 38.37%, respectively. The non-performing loan was RMB 4.233 billion Yuan and the non-performing loan ratio was 1.23%. The provision coverage was 240.83% which was better than the industry average; the loan provisioning rate was 2.95%, 0.36 percentage points higher than a year ago.

4.3 非银行金融机构(Non-bank Financial Intermediaries)

非银行金融机构是除商业银行和专业银行以外的所有金融机构。主要包括信托、证券、保险、融资租赁等机构以及农村信用社、财务公司等。

Non-bank financial intermediaries refer to all the financial institutions except commercial banks and specialized banks，mainly including trusts，securities，insurance companies，finance lease companies and rural credit cooperatives and finance companies and so on.

非银行金融机构是随着金融资产多元化、金融业务专业化而产生的。早期的非银行金融机构大多同商业银行有着密切的联系。1681 年,在英国成立了世界上第一家保险公司。1818 年,美国产生了信托投资机构。1849 年,德国创办了世界上第一家农村信用社。20 世纪初,证券业务和租赁业务迅速发展,产生了一大批非银行性的金融机构。第二次世界大战后,非银行金融机构逐步形成独立的体系。例如证券业,美国有 7000 多家证券公司,18 家全国性的证券交易所。20 世纪 70 年代以来,金融创新活动不断涌现,非银行金融机构起了主要作用,它有力地推动了金融业务的多元化、目标化和证券化,使得各类金融机构的业务日益综合化,银行机构与非银行金融机构的划分越来越不明显,非银行金融机构自身的业务分类也日趋融合。它们之间业务交叉进行,只是比重有所差别。

Non-bank financial intermediaries came into existence due to the diversification of financial assets and the specialization of financial businesses. The early non-bank financial intermediaries usually had close relations with commercial banks. In 1681 the first insurance company of the world was set up in the Great Britain and in 1818 trust investment companies came into being in America. In 1849 the world's first rural credit cooperative was established in Germany. The businesses of securities and leasing also developed rapidly at the beginning of the 20th century and thus appeared a large number of non-bank financial intermediaries. After the Second World War，non-bank financial intermediaries gradually formed their independent system such as securities，with more than 7000 companies in America among which 18 were national companies. Since the 1970s，financial creative activities had sprung up constantly，non-bank financial intermediaries also played an important role and effectively promoted the diversification，targeting and securitization of financial businesses，making the increasing integration of the businesses of different financial institutions. Therefore，the division of bank indermediries and non-bank financial intermediaries became more and more inconspicuous and the business categories of non-bank financial intermediaries also blended day by day. The businesses of the two kinds of financial institutions had overlapping operations except the difference in their proportions.

摩根士丹利（Morgan Stanley）

摩根士丹利（NYSE：MS），财经界俗称"大摩"，是一家成立于美国纽约的全球领先的国际金融服务公司，业务范围涵盖投资银行、证券、投资管理以及财富管理等。目前公司在全球 37 个国家设有超过 1200 家办事处，雇员总数达 5 万多人，公司员工竭诚为各地企业、政府机关、事业机构和个人投资者提供服务。2008 年 9 月，更改公司注册地位为"银行控股公司"。

Morgan Stanley（NYSE：MS）, commonly known as JP Morgan in economic and financial circles, is a globally-leading international financial service company founded in New York, America. The business scope of Morgan Stanley covers investment bank, securities, investment management, wealth management and so on. The company has set up more than 1200 agencies in thirty-seven countries around the world up to now with a total number of over 50000 employees who provide services whole heartedly for enterprises, government agencies, institutional organizations and individual investors. Its registry status was changed to bank holding company in September, 2008.

摩根士丹利是最早进入中国发展的国际投资银行之一，多年来业绩卓越。在 2016 年财富世界 500 强排行榜中排名第 263 位，在美国 500 强排行榜中公司排名第 78 位。摩根士丹利总公司下设 9 个部门，包括股票研究部、投资银行部、私人财富管理部、外汇/债券部、商品交易部、固定收益研究部、投资管理部、直接投资部和机构股票部。

Morgan Stanley, with outstanding performance for many years, was one of the first international investment banks developing in China. It ranked No. 263 of Fortune Global 500 and No. 78 of US Fortune 500 in 2016. The head office of Morgan Stanley consists of nine departments such as Stocks Research Department, Investment Banking Department, Private Wealth Management Department, Forex and Bond Department, Commodity Trade Department, Fixed-income Research Department, Investment Mangement Department, Direct Investment Department and Institution Equities Department.

　　摩根士丹利国际银行（中国）有限公司是摩根士丹利集团的子公司摩根士丹利国际银行有限公司的全资附属机构，总部位于上海市浦东新区。公司在华主要业务分为证券业务和投资管理业务两大类。

　　Headquartered in Pudong New Area of Shanghai, Morgan Stanley Bank International Limited （China） is the wholly owned subsidiary of Morgan Stanley Bank International Limited which is also a branch of Morgan Stanley. The company is mainly engaged in securities and investment management in China.

　　摩根士丹利在亚太区有雇员 2000 余人，其中有约 1500 人在大中华区（中国内地、港澳和台湾）工作，在香港、北京、上海和台北设有办事处。1995 年 8 月，摩根士丹利与中国建设银行合资组建中国国际金融有限公司，公司目前控股 49%。摩根士丹利也因此成为首家在中国内地建立合资投资银行的国际金融公司。通过在中国的合资银行，摩根士丹利得以为许多中国公司提供在海外上市的服务，包括中国联通、中石化和中国电信等，筹得的总资金超过 100 亿美元。

　　Morgan Stanley has more than 2000 employees in APAC （Asia Pacific） among whom about 1500 work in Greater China （including Chinese Mainland, Hong Kong and Macao, Taiwan）. It also sets up agencies in Hong Kong, Beijing, Shanghai and Taipei. Morgan Stanley together with the China Construction Bank set up China International Capital Corporation Ltd. in August, 1995 with a present holding of 49 percent. Thus, Morgan Stanley became the first international finance corporation to establish joint-ventured investment bank in Chinese mainland. By means of joint-ventured banks in China, Morgan Stanley can provide overseas listing services for many Chinese companies, including China Unicom, Sinopec, China Telecom and so on with total capital raised over 10 Billion US Dollars.

高盛集团（Goldman Sachs）

　　高盛集团为跨国银行控股公司集团，成立于 1869 年，总部位于美国纽约，连续多年被《财富》杂志评选为世界财富 500 强企业之一。其业务涵盖投资银行、证券交易和财富管理；业务对象为企业、金融机构、（国家）政府及富人；业务按地域分为三大块，即美国、亚太地区和欧洲。在 19 世纪 90 年代到第一次世界大战期间，投资银行业务开始形成，但与商业银行没有区分。高盛公司在此阶段最初从事商业票据交易,创业时只有一个办公人员和一个兼职记账员。创始人马可斯·戈德门每天沿街打折收购商人们的本票,然后在某个约定日期里由原出售本票的商人按票面金额支付现金,其中差额便是马可斯的收入。

Goldman Sachs Group Inc. (Goldman Sachs), founded in 1869 and headquartered in New York, America, is a multinational bank holding company group which was elected as one of the world's Fortune 500 companies for years by the *Fortune*. Its businesses cover investment banking, securities trading and wealth management. It provides services for enterprises, financial institutions, (national) governments and the rich all over the United States of America, Asia-pacific region and Europe. Goldman Sachs' investment bank business without many differences from those of commercial banks came into being between the 1890s and the First World War. At that time, Goldman Sachs first engaged in commercial paper even with only one office staff and a part-time bookkeeper during its start-up period. Marcus Goldstone, founder of the company, purchased the promissory notes of the merchants with discounts along the street every day, and then asked the merchants who originally sold the notes to pay cash by the par value on a certain agreed date, the difference between the two prices was Marcus's income.

股票包销业务使高盛从濒临倒闭转为迅速膨胀。后来高盛增加贷款、外汇兑换及新兴的股票包销业务,规模虽小,却是已具雏形。而股票包销业务使高盛变成了真正的投资银行。

Stock underwriting business made Goldman Sachs rapidly expanded even from the verge of close-down. Later, Goldman increased lending, foreign exchange and emerging stock underwriting businesses, though on a small scale, they started to take shape and among which stock underwriting business helped Goldman Sachs become a real investment bank in the world.

高盛长期以来视中国为重要市场,自 20 世纪 90 年代初就把中国作为全球业务发展的重点地区。高盛于 1984 年在香港设亚太地区总部,又于 1994 年分别在北京和上海开设代表处,正式进驻中国内地市场。此后,高盛在中国逐步建立起强大的国际投资银行业务分支机构,向中国政府和国内占据行业领导地位的大型企业提供全方位的金融服务。高盛是第一家获得上海证券交易所 B 股交易许可的外资投资银行,也是首批获得 QFII 资格的外资机构之一,并多次在中国政府的大型全球债务发售交易中担任顾问及主承销商。高盛还是第一家中标协助中国处理不良资产的外资机构，也是第一家完成不良资产国际销售的外资机构。

Goldman Sachs has considered China as its significant market for a long time and taken China as the key area of its global business development since the early 1990s. Goldman Sachs established the headquarter of Asia-Pacific region in Hong Kong in 1984 and representative offices in Beijing and Shanghai in 1994, marking its official entry to Chinese mainlard market. Afterwards, Goldman Sachs gradually set up powerful branches of its international investment banking businesses, providing all-round financial services for Chinese government and the leading large-scale enterprises in China. Goldman Sachs was the first foreign-funded investment bank to get the permission to trade company B shares from Shanghai Stock Exchange (SSE). It is also one of the first foreign institutions to have qualification for QFII, and acts as advisers and lead underwriters repeatedly in the Chinese government's large-scale global debt sale transactions. Goldman is still the first foreign institution who won the bid to assist China to deal with non-performing assets, as well as the first foreign institution to complete international sales of non-performing assets.

安联（Allianz）

安联保险集团于 1890 年在德国柏林成立，至今已有 120 多年的历史，现总部设于德国巴伐利亚州首府慕尼黑市，是目前德国最大的金融集团，也是欧洲最大型的金融集团之一。1890 年 Wilhelm Finck 和 Carl Thieme 两位德国人在柏林市共同创立了安联保险公司。创业伊始，安联就十分注重业务的创新性，积极设计新险种，现在的一些保险品种就是由安联开创的。

Allianz, founded in 1890 in Berlin, Germany, has a long history of more than 120 years. With the Headquarters in Munich City, capital of Bavaria, Germany, Allianz is the largest financial group in Germany and also one of Europe's biggest financial groups. In 1890, two germans named Wilhelm Finck and Carl Thieme together founded the Allianz Insurance Company in Berlin. At its beginning of entrepreneurship, Allianz payed great attention to the innovation of the business, actively designed new types of insurance. Many types of insurance were initiated by Allianz.

作为一家世界领先的综合性保险和资产管理公司,安联集团的业务遍及所有金融领域,范围包括寿险、健康险、财产险和责任险,再保险领域中所有险种以及风险管理咨询,并在全球范围内为机构和个人投资者提供资产管理服务。除人身保险、财产保险和资产管理等主要业务之外,安联集团还致力于为客户提供更全面的风险管理服务。截至2015年年底,全世界约有15万名安联集团的员工在为客户提供服务。

As a leading comprehensive insurance company and assets management company in the world, Allianz expands its businesses to all the financial fields including all lines of life, health, property, liability, reinsurance and risk management consultancy, it also provides assets management services for insitutions and individual investor worldwide. Besides the above-mentioned businesses, Allianz also devotes itself to more comprehensive risk management services for its customers. There had been almost 150000 employees who provide services for the customers up to the end of 2015.

安联集团是欧洲最大的保险公司,财产险保费收入长期位居全球第一,寿险保费收入亦排名全球前列,部分年度的综合保费收入位居全球首位,是全球最大的保险公司之一。同时,资产管理业务已成为安联集团发展的重要业务之一。公司通过并购等一系列手段,现已跻身于世界五大资产管理集团。旗下拥有 PIMCO、德盛安联等著名投资公司,业务主要分布于欧洲、美国和亚太部分地区。

Being the biggest insurance company in Europe and one of the biggest insurance companies in the world, Allianz ranks first for a long time in the world in premium income of property insurance, the premium income of life insurance also ranks the top of the annual comprehensive premium income in the world. At the same time, the asset management business has become one of the important businesses of Allianz group. Through a series of means of mergers and acquisitions, Allianz has become one of the five world's largest assets management groups, owning several world famous investment companies such as PIMCO, Allianz Dresdner and so on, with the businesses mainly distributed in Europe, America and parts of Asia Pacific.

中德安联人寿保险有限公司是德国安联保险集团与中国中信信托有限责任公司共同合资组建的人寿保险公司,于1999年1月25日在上海正式开业,是中国第一家获准成立的中欧合资保险公司。注册资本为20亿元人民币,其中德国安联保险公司拥有 51% 的股份，中信信托公司拥有 49% 的股份。凭借安联百年国际金融及风险管理专长，与中信信托本土金融领域经验的深度结合，中德安联以创新的度身定制保险方案、专业的培训系统和诚信的服务理念享誉市场。通过营销员团队、合作银行、多元化渠道和在线销售等全方位的营销网络，中德安联为中国客户提供专业和优质的保险金融产品及服务，业务范围覆盖人寿、养老、投资、教育、医疗、意外等各个领域，全方位地满足客户的需求。

Allianz China Life（AZCL）is a joint venture life insurance company formed by Allianz SE, the German financial services conglomerate, and CITIC Trust. The company was the first European joint venture insurer in China, officially opened in Shanghai on January 25, 1999. At present, Allianz China Life has registered capital of RMB 2 billion Yuan, of which Allianz SE owns a 51% stake and CITIC Trust owns 49%. Combining the best of international financial and risk management from Allianz with local financial management and financial expertise from CITIC, Allianz China Life has earned a strong reputation for its customized products, professional training and trustworthy service. The company offers all lines of life, retirement, investment, education, health and accident insurance products and services through agency teams, banks, and alternative business channels to meet the comprehensive needs of customers.

美国国际集团（American International Group，AIG）

美国国际集团是一家以美国为基地的国际性跨国保险及金融服务机构集团，总部设于纽约市的美国国际大厦。集团在英国的总部位于伦敦的芬丘奇街，欧洲大陆的总部设于巴黎的拉德芳斯，亚洲总部则设于中国的香港。根据 2008 年度《福布斯》杂志的全球 2000 大跨国企业名单，AIG 在全世界排名第 18 位，自 2004 年 4 月 8 日开始一直都是道琼斯工业平均指数的成份股，直到因遭受金融海啸的冲击而于 2008 年 9 月 22 日被除名。

American International Group（AIG）is an American-based group of international transnational insurance and financial service institution, headquartered at American International in New York. Its British headquarters is located in Fenchurch Street in London, European headquarters in La Défense in Paris, and Asian headquarters in Hong Kong. AIG ranked the eighteenth in the world's 2000 large transnational enterprises according to *Forbes* (2008). AIG had been the constituent stock of Dow Jones Industries Average Index (DJIA) from April 8, 2004 until its removal from the rollson on September 22, 2008 due to the financial tsunami.

美国国际集团的历史可以追溯至 1919 年,当时集团的创办人施德于中国上海成立一家保险代理公司美亚保险,提供火险和水险保障。施德是首位把保险概念带给上海华人的西方人。1921 年,施德成立友邦人寿保险,并在短短十年内把事业扩展至全中国及东南亚地区;1926 年,AIG 在美国的纽约开设分公司。当他在中国大陆的保险事业获得成功后,又于 1931 年在香港成立四海保险公司,然后将业务扩展到欧洲和中东。由于日本侵华战争爆发,施德把公司总部从上海迁往美国,进而开拓拉丁美洲市场。

The history of AIG could be traced back to 1919 when its founder Cornelius Vander Starr set up an insurance company agency named AIU Insurance Company in Shanghai to provide the protection against fire risk and water risk. Starr was the first westerner who brought the conception of insurance to Ethnic Chinese in Shanghai. In 1921, Starr established Asia Life Insurance Company and extended businesses to the whole China and Southeast Asia in as few as ten years. In 1926, AIG set up a branch office in New York, America. He also set up Universal Insurance Company in Hong Kong when he succeeded in Mainland China, and then the branches were set up from Europe to the Middle East. Because of the Japanese War of Aggression Against China, Starr moved the headquarters from Shanghai to America and then further developed the markets in Latin America.

中国人民保险集团股份有限公司(The People's Insurance Company of China, PICC)

中国人民保险集团股份有限公司(简称"中国人保")是一家综合性保险(金融)公司,是目前世界上最大的保险公司之一,注册资本为 306 亿元人民币,在全球保险业中属于实力非常雄厚的公司。目前旗下拥有人保财险、人保资产、人保健康、人保寿险、人保投资、人保资本、人保香港、中盛国际等十余家专业子公司。

The People's Insurance Company of China Limited (abbreviated as PICC), a comprehensive insurance (finance) company, and one of the largest and well-funded insurance companies in the world with the registered capital of RMB 30. 6 billion. PICC now possesses more than ten subordinate companies such as PICC Property Company，PICC Asset Management Company Limited，PICC Health Company，PICC Life Insurance Company，PICC Investment Holding Company Limited，PICC Capital Investment Management Company Limited，PICC Asset Management Company Limited（Hong Kong）and Zhongsheng International Insurance Brokers Co. , Ltd. and so on.

迄今，PICC 品牌已有 60 多年的历史，在国内享有显著声誉，在国际上具有一定影响。人保财险是全球各大船东协会在中国的保赔通讯代理，在国际保险市场享有良好声誉。特别是公司在海外上市后，PICC 进一步成为国内、国际保险市场和资本市场的知名品牌。

With a history of more than sixty years, PICC enjoys a good reputation at home and a certain influence abroad. PICC Property Company，who enjoys a good reputation in the international insurance market，is the communication agency of the world's major ship owners association of protection and indemnity （P&I）in China. PICC further becomes a well-known brand both in domestic and international insurance market especially after the company listed abroad.

5 百姓理财
（Personal Financing）

5.0 导言（Introduction）

近年来，我国居民财富正进入一个快速增长的阶段，随之而来的是老百姓对于投资理财、财富管理、保险等金融服务需求旺盛。正在实际操作金融理财的家庭也越来越多。但对于很多百姓而言，理财工具究竟有哪些，又应该如何去应用，确实令人头疼。正所谓"知己知彼，百战不殆"，因而对于"财性"的了解也极为重要。

In recent years, domestic wealth in China has entered into a stage of rapid growth. This is driving the Chinese people's demand for financial services including investment, wealth management, insurance, etc. More and more families are getting touch with finance and getting confused that how to use the financial management tools correctly. Knowing well about finance is also an important matter.

5.1 股票与债券（Stocks and Bonds）

股票，从投资人的角度看，股票是股份有限公司在筹集资本时向出资人发行的股份凭证，代表着其持有者（即股东）对股份公司的所有权。

From the view of investors, the stock is a certificate issued by share-limited company, in order to raise capital from the investors. It represents the ownership of shares of the company.

股东,持有股票就是公司的股东,拥有自身股份所占比例的资产权利,能将该股份抵押、转让,能参与公司的经营决策,按照所占比例进行投票。

Shareholder is the person who holds the stock, has property rights with its own shares by proportion and the shareholder can mortgage, transfer and participate in the company management and vote.

股票面值,是用来表明每一张股票所包含的资本数额,作为确定股东权利的依据,仅代表股东在股份公司中所占有的比例。

The value of the stock is used to show the capital of each stock, on behalf of shareholder's proportion in the company.

股票市场,是发行和买卖股票的场所。习惯上,人们把股票市场简称为"股市"。

The stock market is the place where the issuance and exchange of stocks take place. Usually, we call stock market as stock for short.

投资股市需要了解很多信息,投资者还得考虑各种因素,例如:经济中的增长缓慢或经济衰退时期、通货膨胀指数、利率及其他事情都将影响所投资公司的经营状况。投资者可以向股票经纪人咨询如何选择股票投资,就是说或者选择长期投资或者购买有希望快速获得大笔股利的股票,然后将其卖掉获利。

An investing in stock needs to know a lot of information. The investors also have to consider various factors, such as in the economy a slowdown or a recession, inflation index, interest rate and other things which affect the companies you invest in. The investors can get some advice from a broker for investment option, that means to choose either long term investments or buy stocks which promise a good, rapid growth rate and reselling them at a profit.

市盈率,是基本面分析中的一个重要指标,是每股市价与上一年每股税后利润之比。它是最常用来评价股价水平是否合理的一个重要指标。不同行业的市盈率是不同的,高市盈率的公司比低市盈率的公司的潜在收益大,但是也面临更多的不稳定性和风险。

Price-to-Earnings ratio（PE ratio）is an important index in fundamental analysis, calculated by dividing the market price of stock by its annual earnings per share. PE ratio is a key ratio used to determine how the market is pricing a company's stock. It is different in each industry. Company with a higher PE ratio has greater earnings potential than low PE ratio stocks, but also are more volatile and somewhat riskier investments.

理财百科：股票历史、起源与发展
Financial Encyclopedia：History, Origin and Development of Stock

股票至今已有将近 400 年的历史，它伴随着股份公司的出现而出现。世界上最早的股份有限公司制度诞生于 1602 年荷兰成立的东印度公司。股份公司这种企业组织形态出现以后，很快为资本主义国家广泛利用，成为资本主义国家企业组织的重要形式之一。股份公司的大量出现，产生了买卖交易转让股票的需求。这样，就带动了股票市场的出现和形成，并促进了股票市场的完善和发展。1611 年，东印度公司的股东们在阿姆斯特丹股票交易所就进行着股票交易，并且后来有了专门的经纪人撮合交易。阿姆斯特丹股票交易所成了世界上第一个股票市场。

The stock has a history of almost 400 years, accompanied by the emergence of the joint-stock company. In 1602 the first system of company limited by shares was born in Holland with the establishment of the East India Company. This kind of the corporation organization form was extensively and quickly adopted by other capitalist countries, moreover, further became one of the important forms of capitalist states of enterprise organization. Thus the demand of stock trade increased with the rise of the stock companies, and then the stock market formed, developed and improved. In 1611 the East India Company's shareholders in the Amsterdam Stock Exchange were trading stocks, with special agent matchmaking tradeoff. The Amsterdam Stock Exchange formed the world's first stock market.

债券，是政府、金融机构、工商企业等机构直接向社会借债筹措资金时向投资者发行，且承诺按规定利率支付利息并按约定条件偿还本金的债权债务凭证。

A long-term debt security is the certificate issued by government, financial institutions and corporations that are offering fixed interest payments and promising to return the principal, the investor who buys a bond is actually lending money to the issuer.

Treasury Bond of the People's Republic of China

Governmental Investment Bond of the Industrial and Commercial Bank of China

债券的特性：

The characteristics of bonds：

（1）偿还性，即发行人必须按约定条件偿还本金并支付利息。

Firstly，repayment. The issuer must return the principal and interest.

（2）流通性，债券一般都可以在流通市场上自由转让。

Secondly，circulation. Bonds generally can be transferred freely in the market.

（3）安全性，债券通常规定有固定的利率。与企业绩效没有直接联系，收益比较稳定，风险较小。

Thirdly，safety. Bonds usually have a fixed interest rate. The income is more stable，less risky and has no direct linkage with the enterprise performance.

（4）收益性，主要表现在两个方面：一是投资债券可以给投资者定期或不定期地带来利息收入；二是投资者可以利用债券价格的变动，在二级市场买卖债券赚取价差。

Fourthly，profitability. Investors can get the interest income by investing bonds regularly or irregularly；or can get the price difference by trading the stocks in the secondary market.

按发行主体分类，债券有以下三种。

There are three kinds of bonds in the following in terms of issuer.

政府债券，发行主体是政府。政府债券的利息享受免税待遇，发行债券是为了弥补财政赤字或投资于建设项目。

Governmental bond is a bond which is issued by the government，in order to make up the financial deficit and invest on construction projects. Its interest is free of duty.

金融债券，发行主体是银行或非银行的金融机构。金融债券发行的目的一般是筹集长期资金，其利率也一般要高于同期银行存款利率。

Financial bond is a bond which is issued by the bank or financial institutions, in order to collect long-term funds and the interest rate is usually higher than the rate of deposit over the same time.

企业债券,是由非金融性质的企业发行的债券。其发行是为了筹集长期建设资金。由于企业的资信水平比不上金融机构和政府,所以企业债券的风险相对较大,因而其利率一般也较高。

Corporate bond is a bond which is issued by non-financial enterprises, in order to collect long-term construction funds. With the lower credit level, corporate bond has a great risk but a higher rate.

根据偿还与付息方式分类,债券可分为以下五类。

There are five kinds of bonds according to different repayment and interest payment ways.

固定利率债券,是将利率印在票面上并按其向债券持有人支付利息的债券。该利率不随市场利率的变化而调整。

Fixed rate bond is a bond which the interest rate is stable and printed on the face. The bond holders will get the interest of bonds.

浮动利率债券,其息票率是随市场利率变动而调整的利率。因为浮动利率债券的利率同当前市场利率挂钩,而当前市场利率又考虑到了通货膨胀率的影响,所以浮动利率债券可以较好地抵制通货膨胀风险。

Floating rate bond is a bond which the rate is adjusted by following the level of interest rates in the market. Floating rate bond is close contact with interest rates in the market which is considering the effect of inflation rate, so the floating rate bonds can better resist the risk of inflation.

附息债券,是按照债券票面载明的利率及支付方式支付利息的债券。

Coupon bond is a bond for which the interest and payment is paid according to the instructions on the bond.

贴现债券,又称贴水债券,指在票面上不规定利率,发行时按某一折扣率,以低于票面金额的价格发行,到期时仍按面额偿还本金的债券。

Discount bond is a bond which is purchased below the face value at a discount, and at the maturity date the face value is repaid. This type of bond does not make any interest payments; it just pays off the face value.

一次还本付息债券,是到期时将本金和多期利息一并支付给投资者的债券。

Accrual bond is a bond that you earn interest until you cash it, but you don't get any of the money until you cash it.

5.2 基金（Funds）

基金，是通过发售基金份额，将众多投资者的资金集中起来，形成独立资产，由基金托管人托管，基金管理人管理，以投资组合的方式进行证券投资的一种利益共享、风险共担的集合投资方式。

Funds are a way of collective investment，in which the investors make securities investment through portfolio and share the benefits and risks jointly by fund managers and fund depository.

基金的特性：

The characteristic of funds：

（1）集合投资，专家理财

（1）Collective investment and professional management

基金把中小资本汇集成大资本，有利于发挥资金的规模优势，降低平均交易成本。基金由基金管理人进行投资管理和运作，且基金管理人都是由专职证券分析和有丰富投资经验的专业人士组成的。他们经验丰富，使用最先进的证券组合技术在进行投资操作。中小投资者购买基金，相当于花很少的钱就聘请了大量的专业人才为其进行理财服务。

Funds collect the small capital to large capital. It is conducive to capital's scale advantage into full play，and reduce the average transaction cost. Funds are managed and operated by the fund managers who have a professional knowledge and rich experience on security analysis and conducts the most advanced technology of securities. The medium and small investors spend a little money to hire a large number of professional talents for their financial services.

（2）组合投资，降低风险

（2）Portfolio investment and risk reduction

基金将资产按比例分摊到各种证券，通过适当的分散和组合降低投资风险。基金的多样化投资组合对于中小投资者是非常重要的。基金通常会购买几十种甚至上百种股票，投资者购买基金就相当于用很少的资金购买了一篮子股票。在多数情况下，某些股票价格下跌造成的损失可以用其他股票的价格上涨产生的盈利来弥补。因此投资者可以充分享受到组合投资、分散风险的好处。

Funds apportion the investment to all kinds of securities in proportion and reduce investment risk through dispersion and portfolio. Diversification portfolio is important for medium and small investors. Funds always buy many kinds of securities and when the investors decide to buy the funds, it means they use very little money to buy a basket of stocks. In most cases, the profits created by some raising stock price can be made up for a loss caused by another stocks. So investors could enjoy the benefits of portfolio investment and risk reduction.

(3)门槛较低,共同投资

(3)Low threshold and joint investment

通常基金公司为了适应不同阶层人士的需要,在设立基金时每一基金单位的购买价都很低,有的根本没有投资额的限制。投资者可以根据自己的实际情况购买,从而解决了中小投资者入市难的问题。

In order to adapt to the requirement of different stratum, the price of every fund unit is very low, sometimes no restrictions of investment amount. Funds can be purchased according to investors' own actual situations, so as to solve the difficulty of the medium and small investors entering into the stock market.

理财百科:基金的费用

Financial Encyclopedia: Charges of Funds

(1)销售手续费。基金的手续费分为前端收费和后端收费。其中,前端收费是指当您认购、申购基金时,需缴纳的手续费,后端收费是指当您认购、申购基金时,不需要缴纳手续费,但在赎回的时候再收取,且投资者持有基金的时间超过一定期限,就不用付费。目前国内基金的销售手续费费率一般在基金金额的 1%—1.5% 之间。

(1)Charges for investing funds: Charges can be levied through front-end load and back-end load. The former will require charge levied when subscribing or buying funds. The latter will not have charge levied when subscribing or buying funds, and the charge will decrease yearly with the years of holding the funds increasing. Nowadays, the charge is about 1% to 1.5% of the funds.

(2)赎回费。在赎回时的操作费用,一般在 0.5% 左右。为了鼓励长期投资,一些基金公司推出了赎回费随持有时间增加而递减的收费方式，持有时间长到一定程度，赎回时就可不收赎回费。

（2）Redemption fees：The operating charge for redeeming funds is about 0.5%. It benefits long-term investors, for there is no need to pay this fee if investors are sticking with the fund, the fees will decrease yearly with the years of holding the funds increasing.

（3）基金管理费。支付给基金公司的管理费，目前国内年管理费一般在 0.3%—1.5%，视投资目标和管理的难易程度不同而有所区别。

（3）Charges for managing funds：Charges will be paid to the fund companies. Nowadays, the yearly charge is about 0.3% to 1.5% of the funds according to the investment objectives and the management degree.

（4）托管费。基金的管理原则是"投资与托管分离"。托管机构负责基金资产的保管、交割等工作，同时还有监督基金公司的职能，所以需要付给托管机构托管费。一般在国内，年托管费在基金资产净值的 0.25% 左右。

（4）Custody fee："Separation of Investment and Fund Management" is the principle of managing funds. Depository institutions are responsible for custody and settlement work and supervise the fund company. So we need to pay the annual custody fee around 0.25% of net value of the fund assets.

开放式基金，指投资者可以按基金的报价在基金管理人指定的营业场所进行申购或赎回的基金。当投资者申购基金份额时，基金份额增加；当投资者赎回基金份额时，基金份额减少。

An open-ended fund is a mutual fund which can issue and redeem shares at places designated by fund managers according to their offer price. An investor can purchase shares in such fund directly from the mutual fund company. When investors purchase the fund share, the share inceases; when investors redeem the fund share, it decreases.

封闭式基金，指基金发行份额事先确定，在基金封闭期内基金份额总数保持不变，但可以上市交易的基金。投资者可以像买卖股票、债券那样买卖封闭式基金，当交易完成时，基金份额从一个投资者账户转移到另一个投资者账户。

Closed-ended fund is a type of investment that does not continuously offer its shares for sale but instead sells a fixed number of shares at one time（in the initial public offering）which can be traded on the market. Investors can purchase and sell the closed-ended funds like stocks and bonds and realize that the fund share transfer from an investment account to another accounts.

余额宝是由第三方支付平台支付宝为个人用户打造的一项余额增值服务。通过余额宝,用户不仅能够得到较高的收益,还能随时消费支付。用户在支付宝网站内就可以直接购买基金等理财产品,获得相对较高的收益,同时余额宝内的资金还能随时用于网上购物、支付宝转账等支付功能。转入余额宝的资金在第二个工作日由基金公司进行份额确认,对已确认的份额会开始计算收益。

Yu E Bao is a service that is designed by the third party payment platform Alipay for individual users to create their value-added balance. The users can get a higher income, but also make consumption at any time. You can purchase investment product like funds to get a higher income, pay on the net, transfer and so on through touching your website. The fund in Yu E Bao will be confirmed by fund companies within second working days and the confirmed share will begin to calculate.

5.3 黄金与外汇(Gold and Foreign Exchange)

黄金,一种珍贵的金属,用来作为价值储藏和交换媒介。在人类有记载的历史之前,它就一直作为一种有价值的商品而存在,与其他金属饰品和艺术品一样得到人们的高度赞赏。

Gold is a kind of precious metal that is used as a store of value and a medium of exchange. It has been a valuable commodity since long before the beginning of recorded history as a highly appreciated metal for other jewelry and arts.

黄金投资的特性:

The characteristics of gold investment:

(1)保值:黄金是财富的象征。

(1)Maintenance of value: Gold is the symbol of the wealth.

纵观人类历史进程,无论世界经济如何变化与发展,黄金作为最古老和最普遍为人接受的重要金融资产的地位始终没有动摇过,是当今最可信任的、可以长期保存的财富形式之一。

Throughout human history, no matter how the world changes and develops，gold as the oldest and most important financial asset is generally accepted，and it is one of the forms of wealth of most trusted，long-term preservation today.

（2）避险：黄金可以抵御风险。

（2）Hedging：Gold can hedge against risks.

黄金具有品质稳定、维护成本低、转移便利、变现性强等特点，在发生政治动荡和经济衰退时，价值不跌反升，且作为实物资产可以在一定程度上抵御通货膨胀风险，是一种相对安全稳健的个人投资产品。

Gold has stable quality，low maintenance cost，convenient shift，and good liquidity. In the event of political turmoil and economic recession，the value of gold does not fall，but as the physical assets can be against inflation risk to a certain extent. In sum，gold is a relatively safe personal investment product.

（3）实用：黄金有很强的使用价值。

（3）Practicability：Gold has a very strong use value.

一方面，黄金作为彰显尊贵和生活品位的象征，是重要的艺术饰品材料。另一方面，黄金由于熔点高、密度大、延展性好、传导性强等物理特性，在生产领域用途广泛，特别是在医疗、计算机和航天航空制造业中不可或缺，是重要的工业原料。

On the one hand，gold is one of the important art decoration materials as a distinguished and life taste. On the other hand，because of high melting point，high density，good ductility，high conductivity and other physical properties，it is widely used in production field，especially in medical care，computing and aerospace manufacturing industry as an important industrial raw material.

投资金币，是世界黄金非货币化后专门用于黄金投资的法定货币，一般采用固定图案，每年只更换年号，售价只比金价略高，称为"普制金币"。我国1982年开始发行的熊猫金币就是在国际上较富盛名的投资性金币之一。熊猫金币主要有7种规格，分别是1/20盎司、1/10盎司、1/4盎司、1/2盎司、1盎司、5盎司、1千克，正面图案均为北京天坛祈年殿，并刊国名、年号；背面图案均为熊猫双嬉图，并刊面额、重量及成色。其市场价格涨跌基本上与同期国际市场上黄金价格涨跌同步，其中1盎司熊猫金币的价格涨跌与贵金属价格涨跌关系最密切，投资者可以通过中国金币总公司指定的各地经销机构购买。

The investment-oriented gold coins，specifically for the legal tender gold investment，generally use the fixed pattern，and only change reign title on the coins. And the price is slightly higher than the price of gold, called the "universal system of gold coin". In 1982 China began issuing Chinese Gold Pandas which are famous in the international investment market. The Chinese Gold Pandas coins mainly have 7 kinds of specifications, which are 1/20 ounces, 1/10 ounces, 1/4 ounces, 1/2 ounces, 1 ounce, 5 ounces, one kilograms. The positive pattern is the Temple of Heaven in the center as well as the name of China on top and the year of issuing in the bottom; pattern on the back is two pandas playing together, with the denomination, weight and fineness. The market price basically synchronizes with the international market gold price, and the price relationship between Chinese Gold Pandas coins in one ounce and precious metals is the closest, so investors can buy them from the designated distributions of Chinese Gold Coin Incorporation.

投资金条,是由知名的黄金公司推出的纯金含量大于99.99%,根据上海黄金交易所或国际市场实时价格作为参考价格,可实时买,也可实时卖的金条。

Gold bullion investment collections, sold by the famous gold companies, have more than 99.99% gold content. The gold bars can be traded any time, referring to the price of Shanghai Gold Exchange or the international market.

"纸黄金"又称"记账黄金",是一种账面虚拟的黄金,一般由资金实力雄厚、资信程度良好的商业银行、黄金公司或大型黄金零售商发行,投资者只在账务上从事黄金买卖,不能提取黄金实物,交易费用比实物黄金低廉。

"Paper gold", also known as "account gold", is a virtual book transaction gold which is issued by good commercial banks, gold companies or large gold retailers. Investors only can trade in the bookkeeping. Compared to the physical gold trade, paper gold has the advantage of low transaction costs.

外汇,指用于结算国与国之间国际贸易的货币——字面上即外国货币。外汇交易是对国与国之间进出口商品和制造品定价的方法。通过以一个协定的汇率交换不同的货币,债权人和借款人结算所产生的国际贸易债务,如银行汇票、银行承兑汇票和信用证。

Currency—literally foreign money—used in settlement of international trade between countries. Trading in foreign exchange is the means by which values are established for commodities and manufactured goods imported or exported between countries. Creditors and borrowers settle the resulting international trade obligations, such as bank drafts, bank acceptances and letters of credit, by exchanging different currencies at agreed upon rates.

银行间外汇市场是场外交易市场，这是一个商业银行、中央银行、经纪商和顾客通过遍布全球主要金融中心的电报和电话互相联系的网络。汇率的标价方式分为两种：直接标价法和间接标价法。

The interbank foreign exchange market is an over-the-counter market, a network of commercial banks, central banks, brokers, and customers who communicate with each other by telex and telephone throughout the world's major financial centers. The method of exchange rate quotation is divided into direct quotation method and indirect quotation method.

直接标价法，也称应付标价法，是指以一定单位的外国货币为标准，计算应付出多少单位的本国货币，也即以本国货币表示的单位外国货币的价格。目前世界上包括我国在内的大多数国家都采用直接标价法。

Direct quotation method is also called giving quotation method; it means the rates are quoted in terms of a variable number of home currencies per fixed foreign currency unit. This method is adopted by most countries including China.

间接标价法，也称应收标价法，是指以一定单位的本国货币为标准，计算应收进多少外国货币，也即以外国货币来表示的单位本国货币的价格。目前在世界上只有英国和美国等少数国家使用间接标价法。

Indirect quotation method is also called receiving quotation method; it means the rates are quoted in terms of a variable number of foreign currency against a fixed home currency unit. This method is adopted by few countries like UK and US.

理财百科：外汇牌价解读
Financial Encyclopedia: Interpretation of Foreign Exchange Rate

外汇的买入价和卖出价：两者均是从银行的角度出发，是针对报价中的标准单位外币而言的（例如 100 美元），即银行买入标准单位外币价格对应的人民币价格（买入价），银行卖入标准单位外币价格可以换取的人民币价格（卖出价）。下面以 100 美元为例来解读牌价。

The buying price and selling price for foreign exchange: Both are from the bank's point of view and based on the standard unit price in foreign currency terms (such as 100 US Dollars), which refers to bank buying standard units of foreign currency price corresponding RMB price (buying rate), the banks selling the standard unit of foreign currency price corresponding RMB price (selling rate). Take 100 US Dollars as an example to interpret the quotation.

现钞买入价：指银行买入外币现钞、客户卖出外币现钞的价格。如果我们要把手里持有的 100 美元换成人民币，就是卖出，而银行是买入我们的外币，因此使用现钞买入价，比如我们可以换得 615.13 元人民币（汇率为 6.1513）。

The purchasing price for cash：It refers the prices that the banks buy foreign currency in cash，conversely，the customers sell foreign currency. If we want to change the 100 US Dollars into RMB，that's to sell out，and the bank buys our foreign currency. So the cash purchase price is applied，we can get RMB 615.13 in terms of the base currency of US Dollars(the exchange rate is 6.1513).

现钞卖出价：指银行卖出外币现钞、客户买入外币现钞的价格。如果我们要出境旅游，需要换取美元，就是买入外币美元，而银行是卖出方，因此使用现钞卖出价。比如，我们购买 100 美元，需要 615.13 元人民币。银行通过一买一卖，赚取差价，来作为汇兑手续费。

The selling price for cash：It refers the prices that the banks sell foreign currency in cash，conversely，the customers buy foreign currency. If we want to acquire 100 US Dollars，we have to buy it from banks，and the bank sell it to us. So the cash selling price is applied，we have to use RMB 615.13 to get the base currency of 100 US Dollars at some time. Banks by buying and selling，earn price difference，as the remittance fee.

现汇买入价：跟现钞买入价是一个原因，只不过 100 美元现钞变成了银行卡里的 100 美元现汇。

Buying rate：It is almost the same as the purchasing price for cash，but if the customers has the spot exchange instead of cash.

现汇卖出价：从牌价来看，现汇卖出价和现钞卖出价是相同的，即卖出价。

Selling rate：From the spot selling price，selling rate and selling price for cash is the same.

现汇买入价要高于现钞买入价，因为现钞对于银行来说需要保存运输等，成本相对较高。

Buying rate is higher than the cash purchase price，because the cash for banks need to save and transportation，and the cost is relatively high.

5. 4 理财产品（**Financial Products**）

银行理财产品，是指商业银行自行设计并发行，将募集到的资金根据产品合同约定投入相关金融市场及购买相关金融产品，获取投资收益后，根据合同约定分配给投资人的一类理财产品。在理财产品这种投资方式中，银行只是接受客户的授权管理资金，投资收益与风险由客户或客户与银行按照约定方式承担。

Bank financial products are these products which are designed and issued by commercial banks that raise funds to buy some financial products and distribute the investment income to investors according to the contract. In this way，the banks only accept the authorization of customers to manage the funds，and accept the investment returns and risks shall be undertaken by customers or in accordance with the contract.

银行理财产品的特点：

The characteristic of bank financial products：

第一，与储蓄相比，银行理财产品流动性相对较差，通常银行都会事先规定能否提前终止，终止的日期等，有时客户提前终止还需要承担一些损失。

Firstly，compared with the savings，they have a relatively poor fluidity. Usually the banks make the rules ahead about that if the products can be ended in advance and the date，etc. Sometimes customers shall accept some loss if they end the products in advance.

第二，从风险角度来看，储蓄存款相对是最安全的，一般有国家的稳性担保。银行理财产品的风险要由投资者自行承担。

Secondly，in terms of risks，saving deposits are relatively the most safe generally secured by the nation，while the risk of financial product shall be accepted by investors themselves.

第三，理财产品的收益率只是"预期收益率"，最终实现的收益率要视整个理财期间投资标的的表现而定。

Thirdly，the rate of return is just "an expected rate"，and the final rate depends on the performance of the investment during the whole duration.

银行理财产品分类：分为保本固定收益产品、保本浮动收益产品与非保本浮动收益产品三类。

Classification of the bank financial products: fixed income capital preservation products, floating income capital preservation products, floating income and non-capital preservation products.

保本固定收益产品指银行按照合同约定的事项向投资者支付全额本金和固定收益的产品。投资者买这类产品到期获得固定收益，投资风险全由银行承担。

Fixed income capital preservation products are the products that the banks will pay the full principal and the fixed income to investors in accordance with the contract. Investors get the fixed profit while the banks accept the risk.

保本浮动收益产品是指商业银行按照约定条件向客户保证本金支付，本金以外的投资风险由客户承担，并依据实际投资收益情况确定客户实际收益的理财计划。

Floating income capital preservation products are the products that the banks guarantee the payment of principal in accordance with the contract, but the risk beside of principal is accepted by investors, and the ultimately income depends on the actual situation of the investment.

非保本浮动收益产品，是那些不保证本金收益率浮动（比保本产品收益率高）的产品。

Floating income and non-capital preservation products are the products whose yielding rates of the principals (higher than others) are not guaranteed.

信托是指委托人基于对受托人的信任，将其财产权委托给受托人，由受托人进行管理或者处分的行为。简而言之，信托就是"受人之托，代人理财"。

Trust is the behavior that the grantor gives ownership to a trustee who can manage wealth or handle the benefit.

信托理财的特点：

The characteristics of bank financial products:

（1）投资领域多元化。当前我国对银行、证券、保险实行的是分业经营、分业监管的制度，三者之间有着严格的政策约束，而信托投资的经营范围较为广泛，可以涉足资本市场、货币市场和产业市场。

（1）Investment field is varietal. Nowadays, the mechanism of segregated operation and augmented supervision to banking, securities and insurance business is performed in our country. There is a strict policy constraint among those three businesses. And the trust investment which has widely scope of business, can dabble the market of capital, currency and estate.

(2)可以量身定做理财产品。信托公司可以根据客户的喜好和特性,量身定做非标准产品,通过专家理财最大限度地满足委托人的要求。

(2) The trust company can make the non-standard products. It can satisfy the requirement of trustor according to their favor and request.

(3)具有风险隔离功能。信托财产把委托人、受托人和收益人的权利和义务、责任和风险进行了严格分离。信托契约一经签订,就把收益权分离给收益人,而把运用、处分、管理权分离给了受托人。受托人只能严格按照契约规定的范围和方式进行运作。因此信托理财具有"破产隔离"功能,这是其他理财产品所不具备的特殊优势。

(3) It has the function of risk isolation. Trust investment separates the rights and obligations among trustor, trustee and beneficiary. Once the trust contract has been signed, the usufruct has been separated to the beneficiary; the right of operation, disposal and management has been separated to the trustee. The trustee only can operate according to the scopes and ways stipulated by the contract strictly. So the trust investment has the function of "bankruptcy isolation", and this is a special advantage which other financial products don't have.

信托理财产品:我国市场上可以投资的信托产品主要是集合资金信托。它是资金信托的一种,指信托公司接受两个或两个以上委托人的委托,根据委托人确定的或由信托公司代为确定的管理方式管理和运用信托资金的一种信托产品。由于相对较高的收益和较低的风险设计,这种信托理财产品越来越受到大众的青睐。

The financial products of trust: The products which can be bought on the market in our country are primarily assembled funds trust. As one kind of trust funds, they're trust products that the trust companies accept the commission from two or more trustors, operate and manage the trust funds according to the managing modes which are confirmed by the trustors or the trust companies. Because of relatively higher return and lower risk, this financial products of trust become more and more popular.

5.5 保险(Insurance)

保险,是以契约的形式将大量纯粹风险集合起来,使风险负担得到转移的机制。若被保险人发生损失,则其可以从保险基金中获得补偿。

Insurance is a mechanism for contractually shifting burdens of a number of pure risks by pooling them. It provides an individual or business compensation in the event of property loss or damage.

商业保险,是指由私有性质的保险公司出售的以盈利为目的的保险。

Commercial insurance is the insurance which is sold by privately formed insurance companies with the objective of making a profit.

社会保险,是指在既定的社会政策下,由国家通过立法手段对全体社会公民强制征缴保险费,形成保险基金,用以对其中因年老、疾病、生育、伤残死亡和失业而导致丧失劳动能力或失去工作机会的成员提供基本生活保障的一种社会保障制度。

Social insurance refers to one social security system that under the established social policy, the state imposes compulsory collection of insurance premiums on citizens of all social groups through legislative means to form an insurance fund, and to provide basic livelihood security for members who are incapacitated or who have lost their job opportunities for the sake of aging, disease, childbirth, disability and unemployment.

政策性保险,是为了体现一定的国家政策,如产业政策、外贸政策等,由国家财政直接投资成立的公司或国家委托独家代办的商业保险结构,以国家财政为后盾,举办一些不以盈利为目的的保险。

Policy insurance is one kind of insurance not for the purpose of profit held by the companies established by the country's financial direct investment or the commercial insurance structure entrusted by the country's exclusive agency, backed by national finance, reflecting certain national policies, such as industrial policies, foreign trade policies, etc.

人身保险,是以人的寿命和身体为保险标的的保险。当人们遭受不幸事故或因疾病、年老以致丧失工作能力、伤残、死亡或年老退休后,根据保险合同的规定,保险人对被保险人或受益人给付保险金或年金,以解决病、残、老、死所造成的经济困难。人身保险括人寿保险、健康保险、意外伤害保险等保险业务。

Personal insurance is an insurance that insures a person's life and body. When an individual suffers an unfortunate accident，illness or oldness and become disabled，dead or retired，according to the provisions of the insurance contract，the insurer pays the insured or beneficiary with insurance money or annuities to solve the problem of economic difficulties caused by oldness，disablity and death. Personal insurance includes life insurance，health insurance，and accidental injury insurance，etc.

财产保险，从广义上讲，是除人身保险外的其他一切险种，包括财产损失保险、责任保险、信用保险、保证保险等。它是以有形或无形财产及其相关利益为保险标的的一类实偿性保险。

Property insurance，broadly speaking，it is all other kinds of insurance except personal insurance，including property insurance，liability insurance，credit insurance，guarantee insurance，etc. It is a class of real compensation insurance including tangible or intangible property and related interests.

保险的特性：

The characteristics of insurance：

(1)转移风险：买保险就是把自己的风险转移出去，而接受风险的机构就是保险公司。

(1)Shifting risk：The purpose of buying insurance is to shift the risk，while the insurance company accepts the risk.

(2)均摊损失：保险人以收取保险费用和支付赔款的形式，将少数人的巨额损失分散给众多的被保险人。

(2)Sharing the loss：In form of collecting insurance fees and paying for the compensation，the insurance company shares the huge loss of few people to most of the insured who can afford.

(3)实施补偿：分摊损失是实施补偿的前提和手段，实施补偿是分摊损失的目的。

(3)Paying compensation：To share the loss is the precondition and method for compensation which is the final purpose.

(4)抵押贷款和投资收益：保险合同中也规定客户资金紧缺时可申请退保金的90％作为贷款。如果急需资金，又一时筹措不到，便可以将保险单抵押在保险公司或者银行,取得相应数额的贷款。

(4)Mortgage loan and return on investment: When the customer is lack of money, he can request and get the 90% of the insurance amount as a loan. Meanwhile, if being in need of money, he can raise a mortgage on the insurance policy from the insurance company or the bank to get the corresponding amount of the loan according to the insurance contract.

理财百科:保险的"双十原则"

Financial Encyclopedia: Double-ten Principle of Insurance

理财界有个双十定律,即通常一个人的保险保额应为他年收入的 10 倍左右,而保费支出应为他年收入的 10%左右,上下浮动 5%均为正常区间。保险花费比重过高,会对生活质量有影响;投入过少,则很难保证风险发生时,所得的赔偿金能够抵偿损失。

There is a double-ten principle of finance, namely, a person's insurance coverage should be about 10 times of his income, and premium should be about 10% of his income, while 5% floating up and down is normal. There will be some impact on quality of life if you spend too much on the insurance; otherwise, it will be difficult to cover the compensation for losses.

6 名人茶座
(Celebrities' Salon)

6.0 导言 (Introduction)

放眼历史,我们可以发现很多经济学家在经济理论、政策及研究方法等领域做出了杰出的贡献。而正是这些经济学家的一些独到理念才改变了世界,启发着一代又一代的人们,对整个社会乃至整个全人类起到了不可小觑的作用。他们的出现也为当时的社会带来了改革的春风,他们的研究为人类历史做出了巨大的贡献。此篇章主要讲述了 8 位早期及现代非常杰出的金融、经济学家及他们的主要成功理念。

In history, we can find many economists have made great contributions to economic theories, policies and research methods. And it is these economists' original ideas that have changed the world and inspired generation after generation, which has played a significant role in the development of the whole society and even the entire mankind. Economists' presence has promoted the development of the society, and their research has made great contributions to human history. This chapter mainly tells the eight early or modern outstanding financial economists and their main successful concepts.

6.1 现代经济学之父——亚当·斯密（Father of Modern Economics—Adam Smith）

亚当·斯密(1723—1790)是政治经济学的先驱代表,也因此被誉为"现代经济学和资本市场之父"。而他最主要的两个经典理论分别体现在 1759 年的《道德情操论》和 1776 年的《国家富强的性质和原因研究》中,特别值得一提的是后者,也通常被人们简称为《国富论》。《国富论》被视为当时经济学中最先进的巨著,因为它详尽地解释、定义了自由市场经济,并提出改造社会、使经济繁荣的的方法是致力于理性投资及市场的健康竞争这一说法。亚当·斯密的理念对现在的经济学仍然产生着重要的影响。在他的努力下,经济学成了一门独立的学科。

Adam Smith(1723—1790) was a pioneer of political economics, who also cited as the "Father of Modern Economics and Capital Markets". Smith is best known for two classic works: *The Theory of Moral Sentiments*(1759), and *An Inquiry into the Nature and Causes of the Wealth of Nations*(1776)—the latter, usually abbreviated as *The Wealth of Nations*, is regarded as the first modern work of economics, where he set forth his theory of free market economy. Smith indicated that the betterment of a society and economic prosperity can result from rational self interest and healthy competition. Smith is still among the most influential thinker in the area of economics today. In addition, he made efforts to make economics an independent subject.

斯密的早期生活 (His Early Life)

亚当·斯密于 1723 年出生在苏格兰伐夫郡的可可卡地。他的父亲也叫亚当·斯密,是一名律师,也是苏格兰的军法官和可可卡地的海关监督。不幸的是,亚当的父亲在亚当出生后两个月就去世了。亚当的母亲玛格丽特是法夫郡斯特拉森德利大地主——约翰·道格拉斯的女儿。亚当·斯密一生与母亲相依为命,终身未娶。

Adam Smith was born in 1723, Kirkcaldy, in the County of Fife in Scotland. His father, of the same name, was a Scottish writer to the Signet (senior solicitor), advocate, and prosecutor (Judge Advocate) and also served as comptroller of the Customs in Kirkcaldy. His father died two months after he was born, leaving his mother a widow. Adam Smith's mother Margaret

Douglas, was a daughter of the landed Robert Douglas of Strathendry, also in Fife. Adam did not marry and lived with his mother in whole life.

斯密的成功之路 (Smith's Way to Success)

在大约 14 岁时,亚当·斯密进入了格拉斯哥大学研读道德哲学。而也正是在这个时期他产生了对自由、理性和言论自由的热情和兴趣。1740 年,他进入了牛津大学贝利奥尔学院,但又于 1746 年离开了牛津大学。1748 年,在亨利·霍姆的赞助下,他开始在爱丁堡大学演讲授课。1750 年,他结识了大卫·休谟,他们一起共事并写下了许多文献。其中他们的共同作品涉及历史、政治、哲学、经济、宗教等领域,而两人也因此成为亲密的好友。1751 年,亚当·斯密被任命为格拉斯哥大学的逻辑学教授,并在 1759 年出版了《道德情操论》一书,此书出版之后便在海内外享有盛誉,很多学生慕名来到亚当·密斯所在的格拉斯大学听课。而后他于 1768 年开始着手著作《国家富强的性质和原因的研究》。1776 年 3 月,此书出版后异常畅销,发行仅仅 6 个月后就被抢售一空。

When he was fourteen or so, Adam Smith entered the University of Glasgow and studied moral philosophy there. Here, he developed his passion for liberty, reason, and free speech. In 1740 Adam Smith was the graduate scholar presented to undertake postgraduate studies at Balliol College, Oxford. Then, he left University of Oxford in 1746. He began delivering public lectures two years later in University of Edinburgh, sponsored by the Philosophical Society of Edinburgh under the patronage of Harry Home. In 1750, he met the philosopher David Hume. They worked together and left many workings. In their writings covering history, politics, philosophy, economics, and religion, Smith and Hume shared closer intellectual and personal bonds than with other important figures of the Scottish Enlightenment. In 1751, Smith earned a professorship at Glasgow University teaching logic courses, then in 1759, *The Theory of Moral Sentiments* was published. Following the publication of *The Theory of Moral Sentiments*, Smith became so popular that many students left their schools in other countries to enroll at Glasgow to learn under Smith. After that, he began to write the magnum opus *An Inquiry into the Nature and Causes of the Wealth of Nations*. Later, the book was published in March, 1776, which was an instant success, selling out its first edition in only six months.

密斯的著作及贡献（Smith's Works and Contributions）

密斯在 1759 年出版第一部《道德情操论》后，仍然在继续修改并润色这本书直到他去世。虽然《国富论》被人们认为是密斯传播最广、最具有影响力的著作，但据说他自己认为《道德情操论》比前者更为优秀。他的作品对促进人类福利这一更大的社会目的起到了更为积极的作用，同时它对处于转型期的中国市场经济的良性运行，对处于这场变革中的每个人更深层次地了解人性和人的情感，最终促进社会的和谐发展，无疑都具有十分重要的意义。

In 1759 *The Theory of Moral Sentiments* was published by Smith，as his first work. But he continued making extensive revisions to the book，up until his death. Although *The Wealth of Nations* is widely spread and regarded as Smith's most influential work，it is said that Smith himself considered *The Theory of Moral Sentiments*，to be a superior work，comparing to the former. His work builds a good foundation for promoting human's well-being. Meanwhile，it is beneficial to the sound running of China's market economy in the transition economy，and everyone will deeply understand the human nature and self emotions from it. Therefore，finally it contributes to the development of harmonious society.

除此之外，在这部作品中，密斯辩证地提出了道德的概念，他还提出道德心主要来自社会关系。而他写这部书也是为了解释人类评价道德标准能力的来源，而不是人们与生俱来的对个人利益的追求。在书中，斯密用同情的基本原理来阐释正义、仁慈、克己等一切道德情操产生的根源，说明道德评价的性质、原则，以及各种美德的特征，并对各种道德哲学学说进行了介绍和评价，进而揭示出人类社会赖以维系、和谐发展的基础，以及人的行为应遵循的一般道德准则。

In addition，in this work，Mies dialectically put forward the concept of morality. He also proposed that the conscience mainly comes from social relations. And he wrote this book to explain the source of mankind's ability to evaluate moral standards，rather than the inherent pursuit of personal interests. In the book，Smith uses the basic principle of sympathy to interpret the root causes of all moral sentiments，such as justice，benevolence，and self－control，and explains the nature and principles of moral evaluation as well as characteristics of various virtues，and conducted various moral philosophical theories. Thus it revealed the basis for human society to rely on and develop in a harmonious way, and the general moral principles that human behavior should follow.

《国富论》一书针对重商主义（认为大量储备贵金属是经济成功所不可或缺的理论）做了最经典的反驳，这本书在 1776 年出版后，英国和美国都涌现出了许多要求自由贸易的声浪。《国富论》的中心思想是，看起来似乎杂乱无章的自由市场实际上是一个自动调整机制，自动调整倾向于生产社会最迫切需要的货品种类的数量需求。例如，如果产品供应出现短缺，那么它的价格会上升，生产商因此获得较高的利润；由于利润高，其他生产商也会随即投资生产这种产品。生产增加的结果会缓和原来的供应短缺。除此之外，各个生产商供应增加，也加剧了生产商之间的竞争，从而使商品的价格回到"自然价格"，即其生产成本。一开始并不是有目的地通过消除短缺来帮助社会，神奇的是，问题却解决了。用亚当·斯密的话来说，每个人"只想得到自己的利益"，但是又好像"被一只无形的手牵着去实现一种他根本无意要实现的目的，……他们促进社会的利益，其效果往往比他们真正想要实现的还要好"（《国富论》，第四卷第二章）。

The Wealth of Nations is a classical case to against the mercantilism (the concept that people think that the boom of the economy is based on the reserve of precious metals). After the book was published in 1776, England and America had many inquiries about the free market. *The Wealth of Nations'* main idea is that the free market, seemingly unsystematic, has the ability of self-adjust, and the quantity of the currency will flow to the urgent demand in society with it. For example, if there is a shortage in supply, the price will go up. So the builder will get a higher revenue. This high revenue will attract other builders to invest. The result of investing will increase the production of this shortage supply. In addition, the increase of the supply in different producers will finally have competitions among them. As a result, the price goes back to the "neutral price", the same meaning of product cost. No one is conscious to solve the problem of the shortage in supply. Surprisingly, the problem is solved. Smith indicated that when an individual "only pursues his self-interest", while it seems like there is "an invisible hand", which lead the individual to reach an aim unconscious... They promote the benefits of society, which is better than self-interested goal" (*The Wealth of Nations*, Book IV, Chapter II).

6.2 古典经济学的完成者大卫·李嘉图（Completer of Classical Economics—David Ricardo）

大卫·李嘉图(1772—1823)是一位杰出的英国政治经济学家,他对经济学做出了系统性的贡献,并和托马斯·马尔萨斯、亚当·斯密、约翰·穆勒被认为是在古典经济学上最有影响力的人。同时,他也是成功的商人、金融和投机专家,一生积累了大量财富。当他快退休的时候,他购买了英国议会议员一席。因此他的一生也是充满了传奇色彩的,而最为传奇和值得后人学习的是他的著作《政治经济学及赋税原理》一书。这本书引入了比较优势、保护主义、价值理论等,其中的比较优势也构成了现代贸易理论的基石。因此,他也被称为"古典经济学的完成者"。

David Ricardo (1772—1823) was an excellent British political economist who made systematic contributions to the whole economic system, and he was also one of the most influential classical economists, along with Thomas Malthus, Adam Smith and John Mill. In addition, he began his professional life as a broker and financial market speculator. He also amassed a considerable personal fortune, largely from financial market speculation and bought a seat to enter the parliament when he was nearly ready to retire. His remarkable contribution was the magnum opus *On the Principles of Political Economy and Taxation*. This book introduced the concept of comparative advantage, protectionism, value theory, etc. The idea of comparative advantage was contributed a good foundation to the modern trade nowadays. Hence, he also named the completer of classical economics.

李嘉图的早期生活(His Early Life)

李嘉图于 1772 年 4 月 18 日出生在英国伦敦,他的父亲是个成功富有的证券经纪人,所以,尽管幼时的李嘉图并没有正儿八经地接受过系统的正规教育,但他的父亲花钱给他请任何他喜欢的家庭老师。12 岁时,李嘉图被父亲送到荷兰留学。那时候的荷兰,几乎是全球商业最发达的地区。两年后,也就是他 14 岁的时候,李嘉图回到英国,开始跟随父亲进入伦敦证券交易所学习金融运作,为其将来在股票和房地产市场的成功奠定了良好的基础。

Ricardo was born on April 18, 1772 in London, England. His father was a rich and successful stockbroker. Even he didn't go to any school when he was very young, his father would invite the teachers Ricardo liked and give him lectures face to face at home. When he was 12, his father sent him to Holland to study. At that time, this area was almost the most prosperous commercial place in the world. Two years later, at the age of 14, Ricardo began to work with his father in the London Stock Exchange. These experiences helped him build a good foundation for his future stocks and housing business.

李嘉图的成功之路(Ricardo's Way to Success)

1793 年,李嘉图爱上了一个跟自己家的宗教信仰不同的姑娘。父亲坚决不同意这门婚事,年轻气盛的李嘉图跟父亲闹翻,于是父亲将他赶出家门并与其断绝来往。但李嘉图还继续在证券公司工作,他的聪明才智在证券公司展露无遗,他的事业很快就上了正轨。短短几年时间,他就已经发财致富。在 27 岁那年,一次乡村度假时,他阅读了亚当·斯密的《国富论》,这是他第一次接触经济学,由此对这个学科产生了兴趣。37 岁的时候,他完成了第一篇经济学论文《黄金的价格》,10 年后他在这一领域获得了极高的声誉。

In 1793 he fell in love with a girl who didn't show the same religion with his family. His father strongly disagreed with them. Therefore, he had broken with his father over religion and was hunted out of home. He continued as a member of the stock exchange, where his talents won him the support of an eminent banking house. He did so well that in a few years he acquired a fortune, and became a rich man very quickly. When he was 27, in 1799, he went to have a vocation downtown, there Ricardo read Adam Smith's *The Wealth of Nations*. This sparked an interest in economics that lasted his whole life. And this was the first time he attempted to know the economics. After that, he was deeply interested in this field. At his age of 37, he finished his first economical essay *The Price of Gold*, and 10 years later, he got a high reputation in it.

李嘉图的著作及贡献 (Ricardo's Works and Contributions)

在 1815 年的《论对低价谷物债券利润影响》一文中,李嘉图清晰地解释了报酬减少理法条。1817 年,李嘉图出版了《政治经济学及其赋税原理》。在这本书中,李嘉图整合了价值和分配理论,并且尝试性地回答解决一些非常具有难度的经济问题。而他在阐述古典经济系统上也比任何人更加具体。李嘉图在经济学上被认为是"古典学派",或者说是"李嘉图式学派"。

In his essay *On the Influence of a Low Price of Corn on the Profits of Stock* (1815),Ricardo articulated what came to be known as the law of diminishing returns. In 1817 David Ricardo published the opus *Principles of Political Economy and Taxation*. In this book Ricardo integrated a theory of value into his theory of distribution and made attempts to answer important economic issues,which took economics to an unprecedented degree of theoretical sophistication. He described the classical system more consistently and clearly than anyone before had done. His ideas or thoughts became known as the "Classical School" or "Ricardian School".

李嘉图的主要理论是其著作中提到的比较优势理论。根据这一理论,即使一个国家在所有制造业方面比其他国家都更加高效,它也能够通过专注于其最擅长的领域与其他国家进行贸易交往而获取利益。并且李嘉图还认为,在实质上,国际贸易的基础不是两国生产的绝对差别而是生产的相对差别。这个理论确实可以更好地解释国际贸易的产生。

Ricardo's main idea was based on the theory of "Comparative Advantage" in his book. According to his theory,even though one country is more efficient in all mamufacturing industries than another country,it could still concentrate on the advantage position,in order to get the profit in the trade. In addition,he also indicated that in essence,international trade is not based on absolute but relative differences in production. This theory was a good example to explain the start of international trade.

1500 年至 1750 年间,很多经济学家主张重商主义,而重商主义的出现也提升了国际贸易盈利是为了实现贸易顺差这一目的。然而李嘉图挑战了这一积累黄金或者白银的贸易目的。他在比较优势中提出国际贸易更偏向贸易专门化和自由化。除此之外,他还提出在国际贸易中,虽然贸易的一方比另一方更具有比较优势,但互利互惠仍然存在。而且一个国家应该集中有比较优势的方面去弥补没有比较优势方面。李嘉图的比较优势用数据证明,在国际贸易中即使没有贸易顺差,互惠互利还是存在的。

Between 1500 and 1750，most economists advocated mercantilism which promoted the idea of international trade for the purpose of a nation gaining riches by running a trade surplus. Ricardo challenged the idea that the purpose of trade was to accumulate gold or silver. With "Comparative Advantage"，he argued in favor of specialization and free trade among countries. He argued that there are still mutual benefits from international trade even if one party is more competitive in every possible area than its trading counterpart and that a nation should concentrate on sectors where it had a comparative advantage while engaging in international trade in order to acquire those products in which it does not have a comparative advantage. Ricardo's theory of comparative advantage attempted to prove with numbers that international trade is always beneficial，even when it does not lead to a trade surplus.

与亚当·斯密的观点相似，李嘉图也反对国家经济中的贸易保护主义，特别是在农业方面。他认为实施《谷物法》向农产品征收关税，会降低国内土地的产出并且使地租升高。这样一来，大量的补贴会转移到封建地主手里，而远离工业资本。因为地主倾向于将财富浪费在奢侈品上，而不是进行投资，李嘉图相信《谷物法》会导致英国经济停滞。1846年，英国国会废除了该法。此外，李嘉图发展了有关地租、工资和利润的理论。

Like Adam Smith，Ricardo was also an opponent of protectionism for national economies，especially for agriculture. He believed that the British *The Corn Laws*—tariffs on agricultural products—would cause less-productive on domestic land and rents would be driven up. Thus，profits would be directed toward landlords and away from the emerging industrial capitalists. Since landlords tended to squander their wealth on luxuries，rather than invest，Ricardo believed that *The Corn Laws* was leading to the stagnation of the British economy. Parliament repealed *The Corn Laws* in 1846. Besides，he influenced the theory in land rent，wage，and profit.

6.3 美国银行家——约翰·皮尔庞特·摩根 (American Banker—John Pierpont Morgan)

约翰·皮尔庞特·摩根（1837—1913），即 J. P. 摩根，美国金融家、银行家，同时也是一位艺术收藏家。1892 年,他促使爱迪生通用电力公司与汤姆逊-休士顿电力公合并为通用电气公司。在出资成立了联邦钢铁公司后,他又陆续合并了卡内基钢铁公司及其他几家钢铁公司,并于 1901 年组成美国钢铁公司。他作为美国近代金融史上最著名的金融巨头,一生有着太多巨大的影响,其中最辉煌也最能体现其实力的是,在他半退休时,他几乎以个人之力拯救了 1907 年的美国金融危机。1913 年 3 月 31 日,摩根于意大利罗马过世,其后遗体被送回纽约,华尔街降半旗以示敬意。

John Pierpont Morgan(1837—1913)also named J. P. Morgan, was an American financier, banker and art collector. In 1892 Morgan arranged the merger of Edison General Electric and Thomson-Houston Electric Company to General Electric. After financing the creation of the Federal Steel Company, he merged in 1901 with the Carnegie Steel Company and several other steel and iron businesses to form the United States Steel Corporation. And he did such a huge influence on the American economics nowadays, and the dramatic contribution in his whole life is that he saved the whole financial crisis in 1907 almost all by himself. He died on March 31,1913, Roma, then, his body was moved back to New York. A flag was at half-mast on Wall Street on the day in his funeral.

摩根的早期生活(His Early Life)

1837 年 4 月 17 日,摩根出生在美国康涅狄格州哈特福德城的一个富有的商人家庭。他的父亲是朱尼厄斯·斯潘塞·摩根,母亲是朱莉·珀尔庞特。1848 年秋天,摩根先后入读哈特福公立学校和美国圣公会学院。1851 年春天,他成功通过波士顿英格兰高校的入学考试,这是一所专门培养商业上的数学精英的高等学校。但到了第二年的春天,他忽然因得了风湿病而不能走路,而这个病也严重阻碍了他的生活和学习,于是他的爸爸只好把他送到亚速尔去做康复治疗。大概一年后,他又回到了英格兰波士顿高校继续学习。当摩根毕业时,他的爸爸又把他送到了瑞士沃韦的一所学校学习;当他能够说一口流利的法语时,又被送到德国哥廷根大学学习以进一步提升德语。六个月以后,他的德语突飞猛进,最终也获得了该校艺术文学学位。毕业后摩根返回伦敦。

J. P. Morgan was born and raised in a rich family in Hartford, Connecticut on April 17, 1837. His father was Junius Spencer Morgan and his mother is

Juliet Pierpont. In the fall of 1848, Morgan transferred to the Hartford Public School and then to the Episcopal Academy in Cheshire, Connecticut. In the spring of 1851, Morgan passed the entrance exam for the English High School of Boston, a school specializing in mathematics to prepare young men for careers in commerce. In the spring of 1852, his illness was to become more common as his life progressed struck; rheumatic fever left him in so much pain that he could not walk. Junius sent him to the Azores in order for him to recover. After convalescing for almost a year, Morgan returned to the English High School in Boston to resume his studies. After graduating, his father sent him to Bellerive, a school near the Swiss village of Vevey. When Morgan had attained fluency in French, his father sent him to the University of Göttingen in order to improve his German. Attaining a passable level of German within six months and also a degree in art history, Morgan traveled back to London.

摩根的成功之路及贡献 (Morgan's Way to Success and Contributions)

约翰·皮尔庞特·摩根最早是从一个会计起步的。1857 年,他在当时纽约的邓肯·舍曼公司工作,后来进入了他父亲所接管的乔治·皮博迪公司在伦敦的分行。1861 年,摩根成为他父亲在美国纽约公司的代理人。1864 年至 1871 年,他已经成为摩根达布尼公司和纽约摩根德雷克塞尔的领头人了。这些公司也很快成为当时美国政府财政的主要收入来源。而在 1895 年,摩根对它们进行了优化调整才使得这些公司成为世界上首屈一指的银行公司。

He began his career in 1857 as an accountant with the New York banking firm of Duncan, Sherman & Company, and later entered the London branch of George Peabody & Company. In 1861 Morgan became the agent for his father's banking company in New York City. During the period from 1864 to 1871 he was a member of the firm of Dabney, Morgan & Company, and became a partner in the New York City firm of Drexel, Morgan & Company, which soon became the predominant source of US government financing. These firms were reorganized as J. P. Morgan & Company in 1895, and, largely through Morgan's ability, they became the most powerful banking houses in the world.

摩根从小就显示出了过人的经商才能,尤其在投机方面具备超常的判断力,可以说他是靠投机本领发家的。19 世纪,摩根大肆收购铁路,因为当时的铁路行业异常火热,他便投入其中,并且对一些有财政问题的铁路进行调整与改造。到最后,全美大概六分之一的铁路都是他控制的。就这样他在铁路行业上取得了不少的股份,并一直贯彻他的摩根体制。到 20 世纪中期,通过摩根体制,他控制了美国大批工矿企业,而在 1901 年,他从安德鲁购·卡内尔公司以 4.8 亿美元购买了卡内基钢铁公司,并且兼并了其他钢铁公司,从而开办了自己的美国钢铁公司,这也是当时世界上唯一营业额超过十亿美元的公司。当时的他集中了全美 1/4 的企业资本。不仅如此,在他的帮助下还成立了美国通用公司、国际收割机公司、美国电话电报等大型企业。1902 年,他也参与投资了美国远洋运输公司,而 10 年后,著名的泰坦尼克号就是他 IMM 公司旗下的产物,这艘"海上钢铁侠"却在它的处女航中撞上了冰山,而摩根却因意外地取消了他的船票而幸免于难。

When Morgan was a child, he shows his unique ability of business. His judgment and speculation is very sensitive in the investment. During the late nineteenth century, a period when the US railroad industry experienced rapid overexpansion and heated competition, Morgan was heavily involved in reorganizing and consolidating a number of financially troubled railroads. In the process, he gained control of significant portions of these railroads' stock and eventually controlled an estimated one-sixth of America's rail lines. By the middle of the twentieth century, Morgan's focus had controlled lots of industrial and mining industries at that time. In 1901, he bought the Carnegie Steel Company from Andrew Carnegie for some 480 million US Dollars then merged it with a group of other steel companies to create US Steel, then became the world's first billion-dollar corporation at that time. So finally, one fourth of US corporate capital was centralized by him. Morgan also helped engineer the deals that established General Electric, International Harvester, American Telephone & Telegraph and other industrial giants. In 1902, he was a conglomeration of transatlantic shipping companies. A decade later, the Titanic, owned by one of the IMM companies, White Star, sank on its maiden voyage after hitting an iceberg. Morgan escaped from the ill-fated April, 1912 voyage due to cancelling his ticket.

摩根的贡献还不仅于此,当时的美国没有中央银行,因此他利用自己的影响力挽救了好几次经济危机。比如在 1907 年的恐慌就是一个几乎摧毁美国经济的金融危机。纽约的主要银行都处于破产的边缘，在摩根接手并解决危机之前并没有任何的机制来挽救他们。财政部部长乔治·柯特柳准备使用 3500 万美元的联邦资金来平息风暴，但并没有好的使用方法。摩根接管之后，在纽约自己的宅第与全国领先的金融家们会面，让他们拿出了一个应对危机的计划，并因此稳定了市场。

The contribution of Morgan was infinite. The United States had no central bank at that time, so he used his influence to help save the nation from disaster during several economic crises. For instance, the panic in 1907 was the financial crisis that almost destroyed the whole America. Many banks were facing the bankruptcy. The financial minister George Cortelyou prepared to solve the problem by investing 35 million US Dollars, but didn't have good using ways. However, Morgan held a meeting of the country's top financiers at his home in New York City and convinced them to bail out various faltering financial institutions. Thus the market was kept steadily.

6.4 宏观经济学创始人——约翰·梅纳德·凯恩斯 (Founder of Macroeconomics—John Maynard Keynes)

约翰·梅纳德·凯恩斯（1883—1946），是活跃于 20 世纪上半叶的著名经济学家、哲学家和政治家。除此之外，他对商业循环的原因的深入了解也使得他成为现代西方经济学家中最有影响力的经济学家之一。作为宏观经济的创始人，他创立的宏观经济学与弗洛伊德所创的精神分析法及爱因斯坦发现的相对论被并称为 20 世纪人类知识界的三大革命。1919 年，凯恩斯的代表作《和平的经济后果》一经出版，就在全世界抢销一空。1936 年 2 月 4 日，他的著作《就业、利息与货币通论》出版，此书堪称他一生中写得最好的一本书。凯恩斯在这本书中也倾注了他作为一个经济学家所拥有的热情与才华。因此这本书也被视为现代宏观经济学的基础。他的思想至今还在广为流传，很多国家包括澳大利亚、英国、加拿大、美国均把其理论作为参考标准。

John Maynard Keynes(1883—1946) was an British economist, politician and philosopher, fully involved in economics and politics in the first half of the 20th century. Besides, he has built on and greatly refined earlier work on the causes of business cycles, and is widely considered to be one of the most influential economists. His modern macroeconomics, Sigmund Freud's psychoanalysis and Albert Einstein's theory of relativity are represented as the three important revolutions in the twentieth century. In 1919, Keynes' *The Economic Consequences of the Peace* was published, and it was a best-seller throughout the world at that time. Keynes' magnum opus, *The General Theory of Employment, Interest and Money* was published on February 4, 1936. This book has been described as Keynes' best work, where he was able to bring all his gifts to bear—his passion as well as his skill as an economist. This book is often viewed as the foundation of modern macroeconomics. Keynes' theories are still given great consideration in these countries as Australia, Britain, Canada, the United States, etc.

凯恩斯早期生活 (His Early Life)

凯恩斯于 1883 年 6 月 5 日出生在英格兰剑桥的一个中上层阶级家庭。他的父亲约翰·内维尔·凯恩斯是剑桥大学社会道德科学专业的讲师,他的母亲弗洛朗斯·艾达·布朗是一位成功的作家和社会改革家。凯恩斯是家庭中最大的孩子,他还有两个弟弟。在 14 岁的时候,凯恩斯进入伊顿公学主修数学,其间曾获托姆林奖金。1902 年,他进入剑桥国王学院再次专攻数学,并于 1905 年获得剑桥国王学院数学学位。毕业后,在经济学家阿尔佛雷德·马歇尔的影响下,凯恩斯开始攻读经济学。

Keynes was born on June 5, 1883, at an upper-middle-class family from Cambridge, England. His father, John Neville Keynes, was a lecturer in social moral science at the University of Cambridge and his mother Florence Ada Brown was a successful writer and a social reformer. Keynes was the first-born child, and was followed by two younger brothers. When he was fourteen, he attended at Eton College and majored in mathematics, and during this period he won the Tomline Prize. In 1902, Keynes left Eton for the King's College, Cambridge to study mathematics and got his degree there in 1905. After graduation, Keynes began to study economics with the influence of Alfred Marshall.

凯恩斯的成功之路 (Keynes' Way to Success)

1906 年,凯恩斯通过了英国文官考试,并在英国政府印度事务部担任文官。

一开始他很喜欢这份工作,但没过多久,他就厌倦了这样单调的生活,于是他于1908年回到英国剑桥,并开始着手他的作品《概率论》。1909年,凯恩斯第一次在《经济学杂志》上发表自己的专业文章,讲述的是整个经济萧条背景对印度的影响。次年,他已经成为这个杂志的主编。1913年,他出版了自己的第一本著作《印度的通货和金融》。之后,他先后出版了另外几本著作,并且从事证券投资、获利数十万英镑,还兼任过不少公司的顾问或董事。但第一次世界大战爆发后,他被征召进财政部工作,曾以英国财政部首席代表身份参加巴黎和会并因对德国赔款问题的意见未被接受而忿然辞职回到剑桥。第二次世界大战期间,凯恩斯担任了英国财政部顾问,是英国战时经济政策的主要制定者。在那个时候,他已经是经济界非常著名的人物了。

In 1906 he passed the civil service exam and worked as a clerk in the India office of British government. He enjoyed his work at first, but later he became bored and resigned his position to return to Cambridge and work on his *Probability Theory* in 1908. In 1909 Keynes published his first professional economics article in the *Economics Journal* about the effect of a recent global economic downturn on India. In the next year, Keynes was made chief editor of the *Economic Journal*. In 1913, he published his first book, *Indian Currency and Finance*. Then he published many famous books, worked for security companies and earned more than hundred thousand pounds. In addition, he did a part-time job to be a counselor or director in many enterprises. During the period of World War I, he was required to work in the Financial Office of UK. Keynes was appointed chief financial representative for the Treasury to the 1919 Versailles Peace Conference. He resigned because he thought the *Treaty of Versailles* was overly burdensome for Germany. After that, he returned to Cambridge to resume teaching. By the arrival of World War II Keynes was a financial counselor and policy maker of British economics. At that time, he was a celebrity and an acknowledged expert on economics.

凯恩斯的著作及贡献 (Keynes' Works and Contributions)

凯恩斯一生出版了很多作品,主要包括《凡尔塞和约的经济后果》(1919)、《货币改革论》(1923)、《货币论》(1930)、《就业、利息和货币通论》(1936)等。当时英国的失业率骤增,高达20%,凯恩斯对此进行调查研究并且写下了《就业、利息和货币通论》(以下简称《通论》)一书。而这本书也彻底颠覆了其他传统经济学家的思想理念,引起了真正的经济学革命。他的《通论》一书从很多方面对经济学进行了革新,尤其是他提出的理念:总需求量是所有的消费、投资及政府支出的供给总和(也就是 Y = C + I + G,其中 C = 消费,I = 投资,G = 政府支出)。除此之外,他还指出全部就业只能在有政府支持的情况下才能维持,而且工资不能下降,因此《通论》里他也主张工资应该保持稳定。一旦降低工资,收入、消费和总需求量就会减少。这在原则上和以降低劳动力成本所得的利益是相互抵消的。

Keynes published lots of books in his whole life, mainly concluding *The Economics Consequences of the Peace*(1919), *A Track on Monetary Reform* (1923), *Theory of Money*(1930)and *The General Theory of Employment*, *Interest and Money*(1936, hereinafter as *General Theory*), etc. At that time, the unemployment in Britain dragged on, reaching as high as 20 percent. Keynes investigated the causes of Britain's economic woes, and *General Theory and Money* was the result. This book revolutionized the way economists think about economics. It was path-breaking in several ways, in particular because it introduced the notion of aggregate demand as the sum of consumption, investment, and government spending, which is presented in formula: $Y = C + I + G$. In this formula, C means consumption, I means investment and G means government. Moreover, he pointed out that full employment could be maintained only with the help of government. But he actually wanted wages not to fall, and in fact advocated in the *General Theory* that wages be kept stable. A general cut in wages, he argued, would decrease income, consumption, and aggregate demand. This would offset any benefits to output that the lower price of labor might have contributed.

除此之外,凯恩斯书中的基本观点是社会的就业量取决于有效需求。所谓有效需求,是指商品的总供给价格和总需求价格达到均衡时的总需求。当总需求价格大于总供给价格时,社会对商品的需求超过商品的供给,资本家就会增加雇佣工人数量,并且扩大生产;反之,总需求价格小于总供给价格时,就会出现供过于求的状况,资本家或被迫降价出售商品,或让一部分商品滞销,则资本家会因不能保证最低盈利而减少雇员,收缩生产。因此,就业量取决于总供给与总需求的均衡点。

In addition, Keynes's basic idea in this book is that the employment of the society is up to the aggregate demand. What does it mean by aggregate demand?

It stands for the aggregate demand when the aggregate supply price and the aggregate demand price reach the equilibrium. But when the total demand exceeds the total supply, investor will increase the amount of employers, and then expend the production. In contract, if the price of demand is below the price of supply, hence, the total supply will exceed the total demand, which will decrease the price of products. So the investor couldn't earn the minimum profit and then reduce the quality of employees and production. As a result, the employment is made of the equilibrium of total supply and total demand.

6.5 股票之神——沃伦·爱德华·巴菲特（God of Stocks—Warren Edward Buffett）

沃伦·巴菲特说："人们对于投资的衡量，不是他们了解多少，而是应该知道他们到底不了解多少。对于投资人来说，他们不需要花太多时间去做对的事情，只要能尽量避免犯大的错误。"

Warren Buffett says, "What counts for most people in investing is not how much they know, but rather how realistically they define what they don't know. An investor needs to do very few things right as long as he or she avoids big mistakes."

沃伦·巴菲特（1930— ）是一个传奇，被美国人称为"除了父亲外，最值得尊敬的男人"。他是全球著名的投资商和金融家，同时也是一个慈善家。他曾在2008 年《福布斯》发布的全球富豪排行榜上跃居首位，是当时的世界首富。在一次慈善募捐中，巴菲特的午餐拍卖达到创纪录的 263 万美元。2010 年 7 月，沃伦·巴菲特再次向 5 家慈善机构捐赠股票，根据当时市值计算相当于 19.3 亿美元。2012 年，美国《时代》杂志称巴菲特是最具影响力的人物。

Warren Buffett (1930—) is a legend, and he is also named as "the most respect man besides farther" in America. He is a famous investor, financier and philanthropist in the world. He is widely considered the most successful investor of the 20th century. In the list given by *Forbes*, he was ranked as the world's wealthiest person in 2008. In a charity donation, Buffet's lunch broke the record in the auction, up to 2.63 million US Dollars. Then in July, 2010, he donated the stocks to five charity organizations, again. Based on the market value, it was equivalent to 1.93 billion US Dollars. In 2012, American magazine *Time* named Buffett one of the most influential persons in the world.

巴菲特的早期生活 (His Early Life)

1930 年 8 月 30 日,沃伦·巴菲特出生在美国内布拉斯加州奥马哈市,此时正是内布拉斯加州的经济大萧条时期。巴菲特从小就是一个数学奇才,他的天资在很小的时候就已展露无遗。巴菲特的父亲是一名股票经纪人,因此巴菲特经常在他爸爸的股票公司学习。11 岁时,巴菲特就开始了他人生中的第一次投资——买了三股城市服务的优先股,虽然卖掉后赚了一些钱,但他还是十分后悔,因为这三只股票的股价涨幅巨大。这件事让巴菲特有机会给自己的投资上了第一课,投资需要耐心等待。

Warren Buffett was born on August 30, 1930, at Omaha, Nebraska, the United States during the Great Depression. Buffett is a math prodigy, and he began to show his intelligence and talent as a young child. His father was a stockbroker, and Buffett spent many hours at his father's stock brokerage shop. At the age of 11, He made his first investment, buying three shares of cities service preferred. He sold his shares at a small profit, but regretted his choice when the stocks shot up to a much higher price. Buffett used this experience as an early lesson on investment with patience.

巴菲特的成功之路 (Warren Buffet's Way to Success)

沃伦·巴菲特于 1950 年拿到了内布拉斯加州大学的科学学士学位。读完了本杰明·格雷厄姆的《智慧的投资者》后,他希望拜读于本杰明的门下,于是他到哥伦比亚大学求学,并在 1951 年取得了经济学硕士学位。毕业之后,他回到了奥马哈市开办投资了巴菲特公司,这时的他既是投资商又是销售员。在此期间,教授格雷厄姆也非常欣赏巴菲特的才华,这种深厚的师生之情也使得巴菲特在纽约的格雷厄姆公司得到了一份证券分析师的工作。于是他在这里工作了两年,不断从格雷厄姆教授那里学习和积累经验,为他以后的投资理财打下了一个很好的基础,也为他在成功路上描绘了重要的一笔。

Warren Buffett graduated from the University of Nebraska in 1950 with a Bachelor of Science. After reading *The Intelligent Investor* by Benjamin Graham, he wanted to study under Graham，and did so at Columbia University，obtaining his Master of Economics in 1951. After graduation，he returned to Omaha and formed the investment firm of Buffett-Falk & Company，and worked as both an investor and salesman at that time. During that period，Buffett developed a close relationship with Graham，who was generous with his time and thoughts. This interaction between the former professor and student eventually landed Buffett a job with Graham's New York firm，Graham-Newman Corporation，where he worked as a security analyst for two years. These two years of working experience were instructive that formed the good foundation for Buffett's approach to successful stock investing.

　　巴菲特在 25 岁的时候希望能够独立工作，于是他再一次选择回到奥马哈市，以 10 万美金作为启动资本开始合伙投资。1965 年，巴菲特已经兼并了在马萨诸塞州贝德福德的伯克希尔海瑟威纺织公司。在兼并此公司后，巴菲特使得此公司成功转型，也使得整个公司的财务结构更加优化。1973 年到 1974 年间的市场崩盘中，巴菲特得到了一个廉价收购一家公司的机会。就是凭借这样的投资模式，伯克希尔海瑟威日益壮大，资产实力日益雄厚。

　　Wanting to work independently，Buffett returned once again to Omaha and started a partnership investment at the age of 25 with a starting capital of $ 100,000. In 1965，Buffett acquired Berkshire Hathaway Textile Company in New Bedford，Massachusetts. After acquiring Berkshire，Buffett made a successful turnaround of the company，which focused on changing the company's financial framework. The market collapse happened between 1973 and 1974，Buffett got an opportunity to purchase the other company at bargain prices. Until now，Berkshire Hathaway is a massive holdings company for a variety of businesses with strong assets and capital.

巴菲特的著作及贡献（Buffett's Works and Contributions）

　　沃伦·巴菲特没有写过特定的投资书，但他会写些年度报告和一些零星的文章。他的投资理念，例如"有序、耐心、价值"，一直流传至今，很多书籍记录了他的投资理念及策略。沃伦·巴菲特认为自己最大的价值，是来自资本管理的能力。他主要的责任是提供资本给经济状况良好的企业，并保留原有的管理阶层，继续带领公司成长。2011 年 6 月 30 日，伯克希尔海瑟威公司的现金和现金等价物就高达

490 亿美元。到 2013 年 3 月,巴菲特的资本净值是 585 亿美元。据统计,他完全控股的公司就有 40 多家。除此之外,大额股权由其公司控股的公司也有 8 家,都是世界知名企业,包括可口可乐、IBM、高盛等。近些年,巴菲特也看准了中国广阔的发展前景,2008 年 10 月他向比亚迪能源汽车贸易投资 2.3 亿美元,并拥有了比亚迪公司 10% 的股份,因此他的子公司也进入了比亚迪电气自动化制造行业。不到一年的时间,他的回报率就达到了 500%。

Warren Buffett does not write any special books about investment, but has written some annual reports and various articles. His investing style of discipline, patience and value has consistently outperformed the market for decades. There are numerous books which have been written about Warren Buffett and his investment strategies. Warren Buffet suggests that his value is the ability to manage the capital of the company. His main duty is to provide capitals to the profitable companies without changing their original hierarchy in order to make sure they're growing. As of June 30, 2011, Berkshire Hathaway had $49 billion US Dollars in cash and cash equivalents. Until March, 2013, the net worth of Warren Buffett is 58.5 billion US Dollars. Based on the statistics, he has more than 40 companies, which are full owned by his company. Besides, there are eight worldwide companies whose major holdings are owned by Buffet's company including the coca-cola, IBM, Goldman Sachs, etc. In October, 2008, Buffett invested in new energy automobile business by paying 230 million US Dollars for 10% of BYD Company (SEHK:1211), which runs a subsidiary of electric automobile manufacturer BYD Auto. In less than one year, the investment has reaped him a 500% return of profit.

巴菲特对"最好商业"准则的定义包括:

①有好的资本回报而不是负债

②他们可以理解

③他们在现金流中可以看到利润

④他们有强有力的经销权,因此价格自由

⑤他们也不是天才

⑥他们的收入是可预测的

⑦管理是以所有者为导向的

Buffett's criteria for "wonderful businesses" include the following:

①They have a good return on capital without a lot of debt

②They are understandable

③They see their profits in cash flow

④They have strong franchises and, therefore, they have free prices

⑤They don't take a genius to run

⑥Their earnings are predictable

⑦The management is owner-oriented

6.6 一般均衡理论创始人——里昂·瓦尔拉斯(Founder of the Marginal Revolution—Léon Walras)

里昂·瓦尔拉斯(1834—1910)是法国著名的经济学家,也被称为边际理论先驱者和洛桑学派创始人之一。因此他被后人推崇为"所有经济学家当中最伟大的一位"。而他最大的贡献是开创了人们现在熟知的"一般均衡理论",他的全新理念使经济数学领域的理论研究发展迈出了重要的一步,也为整个社会经济奠定了良好的基础。

Léon Walras (1834—1910) was a famous French economist. He is considered the pioneer of the marginal revolution, and one of the founders of Lausanne School. In result, he is regarded as the greatest economist among all. Walras's biggest contribution is in what is now called General Equilibrium Theory. His own idea made a major step in developing mathematical economics, which also lays a good foudation for the whole social economy.

里昂·瓦尔拉斯早期生活 (His Early Life)

里昂·瓦尔拉斯于 1834 年出生于法国,他的父亲奥古斯特·瓦尔拉斯是一位法国的经济学家和教师,并且在当时就发现了商品价值与商品的稀缺性和人们需求之间存在着潜在的关系。里昂·瓦尔拉斯在巴黎矿场学校念书时做过很多不同的工作,比如记者、小说家、艺术批判学者。但最后瓦尔拉斯还是回到学校继续学习,最终成了一名经济学教师。也就是从回到学校的这个时候开始,瓦尔拉斯投入、继承并且升华了其父亲关于土地改革、税收政策及经济数学的深入研究。1870年,他终于被洛桑学院学术会提名。1874 年,他开始出版他的著作《纯经济学元素》。但是,当时的主流经济学家都集中于英国地区,而瓦尔拉斯所写的法文显然不能得到共鸣。

Léon Walras was born in 1834 in France, and his father Auguste Walras was a French proto-marginalist economist and school teacher. His father found the potential relationship between the value of goods and the scarcity of commodities and human wants. After spending his youth in several careers—he was a student at the school of mines, and at the same time worked as a journalist, a novelist, an art critic, and for several businesses—Walras eventually returned to study and became a teacher of economics. Thus, Walras followed his father's footsteps. He adopted his father's socialist policy positions on land reform and taxation as well as his main ideas on mathematics for economics theory. Walras finally received an academic appointment at the Academy of Lausanne in 1870. He wrote and published the first edition of his magnumopus, the *Elements of Pure Economics* in 1874. However, this location was not ideal. The dominant economists at the time were in Britain, and Walras' writings in French had no significant impact on the rest of the profession.

1893 年,瓦尔拉斯和另一位年轻人帕累托组成了洛桑学派的核心人物,他在58 岁的时候退休,最后在瑞士终老。

In 1893, Walras and a young man Pareto formed the core of the Lausanne School. He retired at the age of 58 and spent his last years in Switzerland.

瓦尔拉斯的著作及其贡献 (Walras's Works and Contributions)

《纯经济学元素》一书奠定了瓦尔拉斯成为"一般均衡理论之父"的基础。在这种边际效用分析的基础上,他认为各种经济现象都是通过数量关系表现出来的,并且互相依存和影响,在一定条件下达到平衡点。然而各种商品的供给、需求和价格都不是独立存在的,它们要受其他商品的供求和价格的影响。任何局部的变动都不是独立的,必将影响到其他局部的变动。只有当整个价格体系中每种商品的供给和需求都相等时,才能形成一般均衡。他特别强调,要确定某些经济变量的值,必须把这些经济变量间的关系表现为函数关系,用方程式体系同时求它们的值。

Walras's *Elements of Pure Economics* led him to be considered the father of the General Equilibrium Theory. According to this theory, he considered that the entire economic phenomenon was based on the variables and equations. These variables depended on and influenced on each other in an equation, then to some circumstance, they reached the aquarium. All of the supply, demand and price of goods were not independent. Any exceed of demand, supply or price would have influence on the new equilibrium. This general equilibrium was reached which means changes in price that would gradually approximate supply and demand until a steady state was reached. He emphasized that there is a equation to calculate these variables.

6.7 微观经济学体系奠基人——阿尔弗雷德·马歇尔 (Founder of Microeconomics System—Alfred Marshall)

阿尔弗雷德·马歇尔(1842—1924)是英国当时最有影响以及主流的经济学家,他致力于对微观世界的研究,即针对每个独立的市场和企业,而不是整个宏观的经济体制。他在 1890 年出版的《经济学原理》一书,成为当时主宰整个英国社会的主流经济学教材。这本书融合了供需关系、边际效用、生产成本等重要概念,马歇尔由此也成为"新经济学"的成立人之一。他的观念不仅颠覆了传统的经济是财富的科学的观念,并且还为社会福利做出了巨大的贡献。更重要的是,在马歇尔的不懈努力下,经济学也发展成为一门独立的学科。同时,剑桥大学在马歇尔的影响下,也建立了世界上第一个经济学系。

Alfred Marshall(1842—1924) was one of the most influential economists and the dominant figure in British economics at that time. His specialty was microeconomics—the study of individual markets and industries, as opposed to the study of the whole economy. His book, *Principles of Economics* (1890), was the dominant economic textbook in England those days. It brings the ideas of supply and demand, marginal utility, and costs of production into a coherent whole. He is known as one of the founders of new economics. He rejected the traditional definition of economics as the "science of wealth" and made great contriutions to social welfare. In addition, the economics has became an independent subject since then. Under Marshall's unremitting efforts, and then it became the first faulty in Cambridge University all over the world under his influence.

马歇尔的早期生活（His Early Life）

阿尔弗雷德·马歇尔于 1842 年 7 月 26 日出生于英国伦敦的一个中产家庭。年轻的时候，马歇尔放弃了进入英国圣公会牧师的机会，决定留在英国圣约翰学院学习数学，并被选为圣约翰学院的研究员。他先后担任布里斯托尔大学校长、牛津大学讲师和剑桥大学教授。1880 年，他担任英国协会第六小组的主席，正式领导了创建英国（后改为皇家）经济学会的运动。马歇尔是英国正统经济学界无可争辩的领袖。

Alfred Marshall was born on July 26，1842，in a middle-class family in London. When he was young he abandoned plans to enter the Anglican clergy and studied math at St. John's College，and was elected to be a Cambridge fellowship. Marshall worked as a president in the University of Bristol，lecturer of Oxford，and professor of Cambridge. In 1880，Marshall became a chairman in the sixth team of British Association. Since then，he led the British（Royal）Economics Society（RES）. Therefore，he is an unarguable leader in British economic circle.

马歇尔的著作及贡献（Marshall's Works and Contributions）

1879 年，马歇尔的著作《工业与贸易》一书，一经出版便在英国广泛传播开来。1881 年以后，他花了差不多 10 年时间撰写《经济学原理》一书，他研究的重要模型包括边际效用规律、报酬递减规律及生产者剩余等领域。而这些研究模型也为其他的经济学家提供了良好的借鉴。因此，马歇尔的模型对整个复杂经济学起到了一个视觉作用，更好地阐述了复杂的经济现象。

The Industry and Trade was published in 1879，and it was immediately viewed as the remarkable writing in many places around the whole England. After that，Marshall began his economic work，*The Principles of Economics*，and spent much of the next decade at work on the treatise since 1881，like the law of marginal utility，the law of diminishing returns，and the ideas of consumer and producer surpluses. This model is now used by economists in various forms using different variables to demonstrate several other economic principles. Marshall's model allowed a visual representation of complex economic fundamentals. These models are now critical throughout the study of economics because they allow a clear and concise representation of the fundamentals or theories being explained.

《经济学原理》一书被看作与亚当·斯密的《国富论》、大卫·李嘉图《赋税原理》齐名的划时代著作。

As a result，*The Principles of Economics* is viewed the great opus like *The Wealth of Nations* by Adam Smith，and *The Principle of Taxation* by David Ricardo.

6.8 美国第一位诺贝尔经济学奖获得者——保罗·安东尼·萨缪尔森 (The First American Winner of the Nobel Memorial Prize in Economic Sciences—Paul Anthony Samuelson)

保罗·安东尼·萨缪尔森(1915—2009)是美国杰出的经济学家,专长于数理经济学、国际贸易等。萨缪尔森的经典著作《经济学》是全世界最畅销的经济学教科书。而他也是第一位获得诺贝尔经济学奖的美国人,被后人亲切地称为"现代经济学之父",美国《时代》杂志更把他称为"20世纪一流的经济学家"。

Paul Anthony Samuelson（1915—2009）was a distinguished American economist. He specialized in mathematical economics，international trade and so on. In addition，he was the author of the best seller economics textbook of all time：*Economics*. He was the first American to win the Nobel Memorial

Prize in Economic Sciences. He was also referred as the "Father of Modern Economics" and *The New York Times* considered him to be the "foremost academic economist of the 20th century".

萨缪尔森的早期生活(His Early Life)

保罗·萨缪尔森于 1915 年 5 月 15 日出生于美国印第安纳州的加里。他在 16 岁的时候进入芝加哥大学学习,后来取得哈佛大学经济学博士学位。毕业后,25 岁的他成了麻省理工学院教授助理,并且在 32 岁时就成为教授。1966 年,他被授予麻省理工系部最高荣誉。在哈佛就读期间,师从约瑟夫·熊彼特、华西里·列昂惕夫、哥特弗里德·哈伯勒和有"美国的凯恩斯"之称的阿尔文·汉森研究经济学。萨缪尔森出身于经济学世家,其兄弟罗伯特·萨默斯、妹妹安妮塔·萨默斯和侄子拉里·萨默斯均为经济学家。

Paul Samuelson was born on May 15, 1915 in Gary, Indiana, America. He entered the University of Chicago at the age of 16, and received his PhD in economics from Harvard. After graduating, he became an assistant professor of economics at Massachusetts Institute of Technology (MIT) when he was at the age of 25 and a full professor at 32. In 1966, he was awarded MIT's highest faculty honor. Samuelson studied economics under Joseph Schumpeter, Wassily Leontief, Gottfried Haberler, and the "American Keynes" Alvin Hansen when at Harvard University. Samuelson comes from a family of well-known economists, including brother Robert Summers, sister Anita Summers and nephew Larry Summers.

萨缪尔森的著作及其贡献 (Samuelson's Works and Contributions)

萨缪尔森于 1947 年出版了《经济学分析基础》,这部著作是在他的博士论文之上改写的。《经济学》这本书首次出版于 1948 年,这是一本以四十多种语言在全球销售超过四百万册,并且成为全世界最畅销的经济学教科书。这本书也是第二本解释"凯恩斯经济学"和如何用经济学思考问题的美国教科书。麻省理工学院经济系负责人詹姆斯·伯特伯发现了萨缪尔森的这本书,并称萨缪尔森作为一个研究者和老师,作为一个站在巨人肩膀上的经济学家,给后人留下了巨大的遗产。1996 年,萨缪尔森获得了美国国家科学奖,当时的美国总统比尔·克林顿也授予他"在经济科学上非常有建树的科学家"的称号。

Samuelson's book *Foundations of Economic Analysis* (1947), is considered his magnum opus. It was derived from his doctoral dissertation at Harvard University. The book *Economics* was translated into more than 40 languages around the world and sold more than 4 million copies. That is why it became the best-seller textbook. This book was first published in 1948. It was the second American textbook to explain the principles of Keynesian economics and how to think by economics. James Poterba, head of MIT's Department of Economics, noted that by his book, Samuelson "leaves an immense legacy, as a researcher and a teacher, as one of the giants on whose shoulders every contemporary economist stands". In 1996 he was awarded the National Medal of Science, and considered America's top science honor by President Bill Clinton commended Samuelson for his fundamental contributions to economic science.

萨缪尔森是为数不多的在经济学多个领域均非常有贡献的经济学家之一。他的主要贡献包括对消费者理论的基础透析、社会经济福利、国际贸易、金融理论、资本理论，以及动态一般均衡理论和宏观理论。

Samuelson is among the last generalists to be incredibly productive in a number of fields in economics. He has contributed fundamental insights in consumer theory, welfare economics, international trade, finance theory, capital theory, dynamics and general equilibrium, and macro-economics.

Reference

[1] HELBRONER R L. The essential Adam Smith[M]. New York: W. W. Norton & Company, 1987.

[2] BUCHAN J. The authentic Adam Smith: his life and ideas[M]. New York: W. W. Norton & Company, 2006.

[3] SMITH V L. The two faces of Adam Smith[J]. 1998, 65(1): 2-19. Tuscaloosa: Southern Economic Journal.

[4] VINER J, IRWIN D A. Essays on the intellectual history of economics [M]. Princeton: Princeton University Press, 1991.

[5] FRIEDMAN D D. Price theory: an intermediate text[M]. 2d ed. Cincinnati: South-Western Publishing, 1990.

[6] CASEK E, FAIR R C. Principles of economics [M]. 5th ed. London: Prentice-Hall, 1999.

[7] VIVO G D. David Ricardo[M]//EATWELL J, et al. The new Palgrave: a dictionary of economics, v. 4. New York: Stockton Press, 1987: 183-198.

[8] SAMUELSON P A. David Ricardo (1772—1823)[M] //WRIGHT J D. International encyclopedia of the social & behavioral sciences. Amsterdam: Elsevier, 2001: 13, 330, 334.

[9] GIEDEMAN D C. J. P. Morgan, the Clayton antitrust act, and industrial finance-constraints in the early twentieth century[J]. Essays in economic and business history, 2004, 22: 111-126.

[10] BARNETT V. John Maynard Keynes[M]. London: Routledge, 2013.

[11] WAPSHOTT N. Keynes Hayek: the clash that defined modern economics [M]. New York: W. W. Norton & Company, 2011.

[12] BACKHOUSE R E, BATEMAN B W. Capitalist revolutionary: John Maynard Keynes[M]. Boston: Harvard University Press, 2011.

［13］YERGIN D,STANISLAW J. The commanding Heights：the battle for the world economy［M］.New York：Simon & Schuster，1998.

［14］SCHWARTZ M. The church of Warren Buffett：faith and fundamentals in Omaha［J］. Harper's, 2010,5:27-35.

［15］BUFFETT W E，CUNNINGHAM L A. The essays of Warren Buffett：lessons for corporate America［M］. 2d ed. Spokane：The Cunningham Group，2008.

［16］WALKER D A. William Jaffé's essays on Walras［M］. Cambridge；New York：Cambridge University Press,1983.

［17］MEDEMA S G，SAMUELS W J. The history of economic thought：a reader［M］. London；New York：Routledge，2003.

［18］FUSFELD D R.The neoclassical synthesis，the age of the economist［M］. 9th ed. Boston：Addison-Wesley，2002.

［19］SOBEL R.The worldly economists［M］.New York：Free Press,1980.

［20］BERNSTEIN P L. Capital ideas evolving［M］. Hoboken：John Wiley & Sons，2007.

［21］MARTIN F. Money：The unauthorised biography［M］. New York：Alfred A. Knopf，2014.

［22］FABOZZI F J，DRAKE P P. The basics of finance：an introduction to financial markets，business finance，and portfolio management［M］.Hoboken：John Wiley & Sons，2010.

［23］威廉·N.戈兹曼，K.哥特·罗文霍斯特. 价值起源［M］. 王宇,文玉译.沈阳：万卷出版公司，2010.

［24］陈雨露,杨栋.世界是部金融史［M］.北京：北京出版社,2011.

［25］罗伯特·希勒.非理性繁荣［M］.2版.北京：中国人民大学出版社，2008.

［26］刘辉.Yap岛 西太平洋上的世外桃源［N］. 都市快报,2012-03-06(7).

［27］中国人民银行.中央银行系列知识：历史悠久的中央银行——英格兰银行［EB/OL］.（2012-10-15)［2016-12-30］.http://wuhan. pbc. gov. cn/publish/wuhan/3250/2012/20121208142011473421335/20121208142011473421335. html.